As Luck Would Have It

A Journalist's Memoir

Bill Thompson

Copyright © 2024 by William Thompson
All rights reserved.

ISBN: 978-1-7361264-4-8 (casebound)

Published in conjunction with:
United Writers Press
Asheville, N.C.
www.UWPNew.com

For my parents,
L.R. and Martha Biggs Thompson

Contents

Preface vii

I Was Born, Then Moved On 1
Mi Familia 3
College Amid the '60s Youthquake 13
Bring on the Working World, or Becoming a Writer 23
Way Up North (in Florida) 33
Doing the Charleston (First Dance) 43
Doing the Charleston (Second Dance) 47
Doing the Charleston (Third Dance) 65
Thoughts on the Art and Craft of Criticism 71
    Let us pause for a sardonic chuckle 76
Arts Immersion: On Being an Arts Writer and Editor 79
53 Years of Great Conversations (My Favorite Interviews) 87
    The Filmmakers 89
    The Writers 104
    The Musicians 107
    Dancers and Choreographers 109
    Artists and Photographers 110
Road, Rail and Sky 113
Today: Freelancing for Fun and (a Little) Profit 123
Publishing Books (a.k.a., Pulling Teeth) 131
Coda 139

Addenda 143
    A: Interviews 145
    B: Quotes to Live By 157
    C: Travel 171
Acknowledgments 189
About the Author 191

Preface

I thank the Fates for making me a writer. There are a lot worse and less interesting ways of making one's way through the world, but I did not expect to be ushered down so many different paths.

Am I a polymath or polyglot? The former, it seems.

A great many people wear, or have worn, a great many hats. I am far from unique. Even so, I'm putting digital pen to paper anyway in the hope some might be diverted, if only momentarily, from their own challenges by reading about my happily misspent life and career. Or at least be reminded that they needn't be stuck doing one thing for eternity.

If there are 4,000 weeks in the average lifetime, as has been estimated, I want to spend those I have left continuing to learn and discover and engage with others across a range of human experience. Not just as a writer but as a person. Creative indolence also figures in there somewhere.

Full disclosure: My life is based on a true story.

There's nothing especially unusual in the enterprise of taking stock of one's life. As the late Barry Lopez wrote in *Horizons*, his exquisite 2019 memoir, "We, all of us, look back over our lives, trying to make sense of what happened, to see what enduring threads might be there."

For my part, I am not sure how many coherent threads I have found, or if things make any more sense to me than they did when I began the writing. I have lived with these memories a very long time now and hope I have not embellished overmuch. Preferably, not at all. I have tried to be reflective when the recollection warranted it, and honest in the telling. And I have reached an age where I can look back and at least attempt to discern some patterns.

For all my 32 years as a book review editor, I grumbled about how unseemly and presumptuous it was for callow pop stars and other entertainers to be penning "memoirs" while they were still wet behind the ears. My only excuse for writing one now is that I am, astonishingly, 75, with a tenuous grasp of detail, and just egotistical enough to think four or five people other than me *might* want to read a book about my life so far.

So this may be more in the way of a short autobiography than a true memoir, though the line separating the forms tends to blur.

Professionally, I fear my work has been largely middlebrow, in part because I wrote most often for a daily newspaper, but also because—let's be candid—I am no towering intellect. Oh, there are spasms of intelligence here and there, the occasional insight, a happy stumble on witty wordplay, a dulcet phrase that comes out of nowhere. Modesty (no, seriously) prevents me from claiming more facility or finesse than is mine.

Even when I specialized as a book and film reviewer I was always a generalist at heart, fascinated by every facet of the world around me. And that is one overarching pattern, or thread, if you like. Of course, that is one of the beauties of books, especially. They are about everything. And "everything" is exactly my favorite subject.

For the better part of 10 years I was an all-purpose feature writer, which meant I wrote about whatever assignment came along. You name it: From politics and business to profiles and education, from profiling an architect or bridge builder to a refugee or ex-con who dreamt of a better life.

Privately, my hard news newspaper colleagues may have disparaged features coverage as "puff" or "soft" news, much as they did sports, but that was because most of them had never attempted it. Our deadlines and the demands on us were just as tough, and often more so. Try writing six articles a week on radically different subjects requiring a vastly wider range of research and preparation. Then try to sound factual and authoritative in the writing without betraying just how shallow and temporary your newfound "expertise" really was. It's a damn sight more complex (and rewarding) than chasing ambulances, monitoring police radio bands or covering city council. That, I can assure you.

But I've also reported hard news, folks. Most of it is important, even if the newsgathering process often is tedious. And it was always curious how many news side folks told me (*soto voce*) how much they envied me the things I got to write about. For me, boredom was never, ever, an issue.

The demands increased exponentially near the end of my years in daily newspapering (1971-2012), when, with drastically diminished staff, monumentally increased workload, notably less space, and a regrettable editorial taste for the trivial, I was dealing with the entirety of the book publishing universe and every writer and publicist trying to get their book covered, print or electronic, local or otherwise. For almost 30 years I had researched and ordered books for review while conducting author interviews and recruiting, cultivating, and managing a corps of in-house and free-lance reviewers.

But by 2010, I was working not only as the book editor but as an arts writer/editor, a job that involved dealing with every theater, music, dance, film, and collegiate company in the area, not to mention every art collective, gallery, individual painter, sculptor, actor, musician, dancer, photographer and more yearning for a small piece of a shrinking coverage pie. Heaven help me if I'd still been covering film as well. That period (1985-2009) had come to a close. Then there were all those savvy department editors who thought how keen it would be for their reporters to be diverted from their real work—research, interviews, writing—to shoot and edit videos, fill in for photographers, and spend hours on social media. Fruitlessly. Managers were desperate to stem the outflow of subscribers (and advertisers) from the paper and were grasping at straws to restore reader interest. These measures did not work. They were abandoned altogether not long after I retired.

All of which sounds like a massive complaint. And it is. But it's only to illustrate the magnitude of it all weighing on some staffers at the time and to solicit your understanding for and patience with all those still at it, trying to do their best under impossible circumstances: too many demands, too little time or resources. Me, I've moved on to low-stress, part-time freelancing. The yoke is gone. The Geriatric Galahad rides on, spavined steed and bent lance at the ready.

The fact of the matter is that I loved the work, even at its most frustrating or insupportable.

I have also written this book for reasons beyond the simple exercise of doing it: as an aid to memory, for the pleasure of reliving events in my personal history, for perspective, for amusement, for the enjoyment of writing itself, and perhaps for others who might read it.

"So few things are recorded," wrote the novelist Javier Marías, "fleeting thoughts and actions, plans and desires, secret doubts, daydreams … how little remains of anything, and how much of that little is never talked about."

I will start by recounting how it all came to be.

Bill Thompson, January 2024

As Luck Would Have It

I Was Born, Then Moved On

Sometimes I associate a period in time with the films of that era. And 1948, my date of birth in tiny Asheboro, N.C., was a good year for movies. Not that I saw any of them at the time. *The Red Shoes, Bicycle Thieves, The Treasure of the Sierra Madre, Key Largo, Red River,* Olivier's *Hamlet, Rope, The Fallen Idol,* Welles's *Macbeth, A Foreign Affair, Women of the Night, The Big Clock, Louisiana Story, Call Northside 777.* A fine haul—for viewing decades later.

Meanwhile, there was all that baby food to ingest—with a steadfast refusal to swallow liver—and the usual infant stuff that evolves into the delights of the sandbox and one's first experience with interpersonal relationships.

Her name was Cathy, a comely age two, given to effusions and an exasperating caprice, such as refusing to return my bucket and pail, claiming they were hers. Not to mention sitting on top of people until they did what she wanted. Sort of like Lucy in "Peanuts." My first brush with a bossy female.

My family moved to Lexington, N.C. after my first birthday, and it was here that I would spend the next 17 years. I recall little from my earliest years, unlike friends of mine who remember much. But by the time I was old enough and stupid enough to smoke rabbit tobacco, I realized I was a pretty good kid, all and all, keeping a low profile and seldom getting into mischief. That is, unless you count accidentally setting a derelict house on fire when

I was six, or eating entire rolls of coin-shaped communion wafers like they were potato chips when I was a 12-year-old acolyte in the Methodist Church (I liked the way they melted on the tongue).

OK, so I *did* play hooky from Sunday School whenever I could. But mainly I was a model boy, good natured and friendly, though a bit shy—a Davy Crockett wannabe (with coonskin cap and buckskin shirt) like most boys my age, who also dug Roy Rogers, the Lone Ranger, and Captain Midnight, not to forget Sky King and the Cisco Kid.

My folks saw to it that I did not run off with the circus. Though I was tempted.

Mi Familia

I've had more than my fair share of the breaks. Sheer accident of birth, for one. That I was born in the peacetime United States to middle-class parents of admirable character gave me an advantage right out of the gate. Anyone who doesn't believe luck takes a hand in a person's fortunes is delusional.

My mother was 42 when I was born, rather unusual (though not unheard of) for that day and time. And I always chided my parents for waiting until their genes were long in the tooth, child-bearing-wise. I'm convinced it's why I turned out so scrawny compared to my father. But I'll give them a pass; they had to bide their time until Dad came home from the war.

All in all, Les and Martha Thompson were an exemplary mom and pop, offering a fine balance between liberal and conservative attitudes. They were generous of spirit and fair, save for the fact that Dad, a salesman, traveled all the time, putting more of the burden on Mom, who also had a career of her own as a county extension agent and educator.

They had met over dinner at a boarding house—Dad a bit of a clothes horse accustomed to attracting women, and Mom, who thought him arrogant and unappealing. I don't know all the details, but apparently he convinced her otherwise. They were married in 1942, not long before Dad was off to war.

Both had warm, loving, outgoing personalities and a measured way of managing discipline, which I did not fully appreciate until years later, having heard so many childhood horror stories as a journalist.

I've been told many times that confidence in adulthood has much to do with being a child who knew he or she was well-loved, that someone older and wiser also had your back. I had that good fortune from my parents as well as from Archibald ("Daddy") Biggs, my maternal grandfather. Of his 10 grandchildren, I'm told I was among his favorites, perhaps because I was the only child of *his* first child. You want to see a happy toddler? See photos of me cavorting in my granddad's lap.

My parents instilled values I embrace to this day. Mom taught me that learning was a lifelong process and the need to apply oneself within sound and consistent work habits. She also championed integrity, good judgment, the capacity to work both effectively and courteously with others, treating all with whom I came into contact respectfully, perseverance, keeping skills well honed, and the importance of contributing. Plus, one credo I grasped but always have found difficult to put in practice: "The greatest tolerance is tolerance for intolerance." Rather glib on the surface, until you pause to ponder it. It's not about giving fools and bigots a pass; it's about trying to understand their point of view and what forces in their lives caused it to develop.

More in action than in words, Dad taught me the usefulness of an ability to improvise, about rising from a setback and having another go, to not take everything too seriously, to recognize that life could be fun, to be down to earth and accessible, to also look upon work as social engagement, to guard my leisure time jealously, and to try to get paid what I'm worth.

As Luck Would Have It

In other words, between them, just about everything of importance, apart from the willingness to love and be worthy of love.

Dad's route took him up and down the Mid-Atlantic coast, selling tile, metal molding, and quarried slate, among other materials. All those years on the road had to be a grind, though I'm sure there were the compensations of all his friends along the way. A former teacher, Mom's work with Davidson County and North Carolina State University had manifest responsibilities. It was not simply about "home economics," but about working with farmers and professional agriculturalists, being chairwoman of the State 4H (Head, Heart, Hands, Health) youth development program, and hosting a home economics show on North Carolina educational television. Early on, Mom demonstrated the capabilities of women in an age that too often disparaged them and their work. She was a professional woman and a *homemaker*—one never said "housewife" in her presence.

My being an only child likely had a lot to do with Mom having been the eldest of multiple siblings and thus having to serve as No. 2 mother throughout her teen years.

Looking back, sometimes I wish my folks would have pushed me a little harder and expected more from me. On the other hand, I had freedom. Freedom to be outdoors, freedom to explore, freedom to play. With my mates or by myself. As the wonderful poet, naturalist, and essayist Diane Ackerman reminds us, few things are as important in youth or old age as play, especially deep play—a "state of unselfconscious engagement with our surroundings" or even "an exalted zone of transcendence."

In some cultures, kids barely have a childhood at all, so strict and all-encompassing are their schooling and family responsibilities. So I was lucky, if not overly endowed with the motivation to excel.

Happily, my periods of conflict with my parents were few, most of them emerging during the late 1960s and early 1970s when, as a college student, I was passionately involved with the political movements of the day. It wasn't so much that my parents did not share some of my political views—though I'm sure it got awfully tiresome hearing me rail against "bourgeoise" values, racial injustice, environmental calamities, and the Vietnam War. It was their concern that I might get myself into trouble.

I didn't. Not really. But I certainly began to apprehend a larger world.

Growing up, I was protected as opposed to sheltered. I've always joked that being an only child is a good news/bad news situation. The good news was that I got all the attention. The bad news was that…I got all the attention. There was no sibling on whom to shift blame for my misdeeds, nor could I claim unequal treatment.

Notwithstanding the occasional bullying any undersized kid gets, I had an "Ozzie and Harriett" childhood. For those who don't get the reference, "O&H" was an idealized (and generally insipid) Eisenhower America TV situation comedy about the carefree Nelson family, each member of which was as bland and undemonstrative as they were "perfect." They dwelled in a world where the biggest life crisis was the malt shop having run out of vanilla ice cream—an early '50s version of *Leave It to Beaver*. As a kid, I much preferred the show *Father Knows Best*, which at least starred real people, not synthetic stick figures (though my own pop didn't always know best).

Like many Baby Boomers, I am a child of television. TV influenced and helped mold my generation in incalculable ways, good and bad, as it has all succeeding generations—reinforcing myths about our country and its place in the world and creating no end of illusions and calls to consume as conspicuously as possible. To this day, I am still parsing the fanciful from the actual, as is most of my generation, I suspect.

But I was no less a devotee of big screen fantasies—anticipating a lifetime as a movie buff—especially Saturday mornings at the local bijou: Lexington's faux-opulent Carolina Theater. It boasted uniformed ushers (in the evenings), a large balcony, smoking loges, and mock box seats along the sides, not to mention a hobby shop next door with a popcorn-making machine. The theater even let you come in with this foreign substance (their popcorn was more expensive), mainly because they knew we kids would wolf down their candies and soft drinks along with the corn.

As Luck Would Have It

Admission was a snap for us: Pepsi Cola bottle caps, the only time in my life that this committed Coca Cola drinker ever deigned to imbibe Pepsi, that wretched imitator.

The playbill on Saturday mornings usually began with reruns of all those wonderful (if cheesy) 1940s cliff-hanger serials like *Rocketman* and *Flash Gordon,* variations on the silent cinema's *Perils of Pauline* which, 40 years later, George Lucas and Steven Spielberg resuscitated with the first of the big-budget Indiana Jones movies.

These short heroic adventures preceded the main event, typically a John Wayne or Randolph Scott Western, but it was the serials I loved most. They were companions to the early science fiction and monster shows on TV, like *Rod Brown of the Rocket Rangers,* which starred a very young Cliff Robertson. Many years later, when I was the film critic of the Charleston (S.C.) *Post and Courier,* I learned that Robertson, whose daughter then lived in Charleston, had visited our commissary to meet with a reporter. Had I only known!

I soon dispatched a short note to the actor (via his daughter) lamenting the fact that I had lost my best chance of meeting a childhood hero, the valiant and redoubtable spaceman Rod Brown. Robertson was kind enough to reply with a note of consolation.

"So sorry to have missed you," he wrote. "Your very kind and flattering letter has finally found its way into my mail kip. This kip bears signs of rider's sweat and pony hairs. I do look forward to joining you when I next descend on your favored land. Meanwhile, my gratitude to you for plaudits ill-deserved."

Never happened, alas.

My own adventures usually consisted of riding my bike with friends out into the countryside and, after my parents built a house when I was nine, investigating the various aquatic and tree-borne denizens of our large forested back yard. About 50 yards downhill from the house a creek ran by, filled with water bugs (those masters of surface tension), frogs, snails, salamanders and crawfish. The creek banks were mostly clay, which I used to construct small fortresses by the water, manning the guard towers with conscripted crawfish who doubtless wondered what the heck was going on.

From time to time I'd unearth such treasures as Cherokee arrowheads, shards of pottery, and sparkling quartz crystals. I still have some of these treasures.

Summer days were spent in a communal swimming pool. Summer and Fall nights brought squadrons of fireflies. Like all too many kids I'd trap them in a Mason jar with holes punched in the top, not realizing the poor luminous souls were just out trying to find a mate. Me, the unwitting anti-Cupid.

If I could have spent all day every day outside, I would have. On weekends, I'd head out in the morning, sandwich and banana in a bag, and not come home till dinner. No one worried about my whereabouts or safety, or needed to in those days. Even the neighborhood German Shepherds, beagles, and Irish Setters ran free, and were chummy.

I always loved the distinct change of seasons in Western North Carolina, where we enjoyed almost exactly three months of each. So unlike, say, Los Angeles, or Boston, or the whole of the southeast coast. I suppose wherever people grow up, their experience of the seasons seems "natural" to them, even if their winter or summer feels like it lasts six months or more.

Stanley Horowitz once said, "Winter is an etching, spring a watercolor, summer an oil painting, and autumn a mosaic of them all." Give me the mosaic and the watercolor, thanks. Though I am a bit of an outlier for a Southerner is that I *like* cold weather, too.

We'd get several good snows in the winter, and living nearby a municipal golf course meant long straight fairways for playing football, and long, descending, undulating fairways for breakneck sledding, a bonfire of old tires illuminating our way and casting long ominous shadows. We do notion of how much pollution those burning rubber tires were sending into the air, but they smelled awful. I used to love walking a particular fairway alone at night, boots crunching in the stillness, surveying an untrammeled blanket of snow, big fat pregnant flakes still coming down even as the moon rose and lent the field an otherworldly beauty.

As Luck Would Have It

Best of all, the neighboring Jordan family not only had a tree house, but a pony, and sometimes I got to ride him in the family's huge, fenced side yard.

When did I enjoy being *inside*? Rarely, except for Christmas—especially at my grandparents in Rockingham, NC., where I'd savor the delights of X-Mas morning with all my aunts and uncles and a diverse cadre of first cousins: sisters Mary Ann and Terry Biggs; brothers Archie and Fletcher Biggs; siblings Billy, Biggs and Gay Love (I kid you not); and brothers Scott and Biggs Porter.

My self-image was only somewhat marred by getting braces. Mom drove me to the nearby city of Winston-Salem to see the orthodontist, and reward my bravery at suffering the torments of Torquemada with Moravian Sugar Cake from an Old Salem bakery. A delight surpassed only by their gingerbread with lemon-butter sauce.

As I noted earlier, Dad travelled for a living, and was a crackerjack salesman, a capacity I did not inherit, though I did manage to approximate his gift for gab as I got older. For most of my life, he was home only on weekends, while Mom juggled a career of service with homemaking—an especially good role model for a young boy.

Both Mom and Dads were good cooks, which was fine when Dad was home, sick of eating out all week on the road. He'd take over in the kitchen, or cook with Mom, which both of them seemed to enjoy. But no matter how weary Dad was, he tried his best to do all the usual father-son things, like fishing and baseball, and building me a makeshift go-cart. But more often than not I begged him to take me to the railway station on Saturday afternoons to watch the freight and passenger trains stop on their way through town.

I'd wonder about the passengers I saw in the windows—where they were going and what they were like—in much the same way I'm drawn to wondering about the joys and tragedies experienced by people living in a home seen from a distance off a lonely country road, a single light burning in the night. Or on a train myself, passing through the outskirts of a city and peering at the residences. *What are their stories?*

Was this kind of curiosity about others part of what led me to become a writer? Indirectly, perhaps. There were more pronounced reasons for that, as the reader will see later. But having boundless curiosity serves any writer in good stead.

We traveled some when I was a kid, most memorably to Monticello and Mount Vernon, Washington, D.C. and New York (for the 1964 World's Fair), with numerous short trips to visit relatives in the Carolinas, and the occasional long road trip to visit my father's brother, Rome, up in Iowa. (Believe it or not, this Romeo's wife was named…Juliet).

This sort of travel did not hold the same allure for my father, who traveled upwards of 250 days a year, as it did for Mom and me. Nor did he ever care to return to Europe, after seeing much if it as a sergeant in the U.S. Army Transportation Corps during experiences in World War II. He harbored no antipathy for Europeans, mind you. In fact, a Belgian family all but adopted him at one point, and he sustained a correspondence with them for a number of years. I think it was simply that he had had his fill of travel.

It wasn't until after Dad died in 1976 (much too young at age 67), that Mom began to do the kind of travel she had always dreamed of doing, albeit in very late middle age. She still had blast venturing to places as disparate as Holland and Egypt, admitting to only one great disappointment—getting within 300 feet of the crest of Machu Picchu and not being able to make it the rest of the way, and, at age 85, with no one able to help. She never glimpsed the ruins. Then again, she rode camels near Cairo, something I've never done (to date).

Mom was always highly organized and engaged with life, and I'll never forget how she exhorted lethargic, much younger residents of a Methodist retirement village she helped design and lived in to get off their duffs and go do things. She was aghast at perfectly healthy people in their 60s being there in the first place, but *appalled* that they were behaving like life was over.

Mom passed away after a mercifully short illness at age 89, having earned the love and gratitude of many devoted friends. During much of her last year, I drove back and forth from Charleston, S.C. to Thomasville, N.C.

to see her on weekends, but I regretted not being in more regular contact with her in her last years. She had always respected (and encouraged) my independence and pooh-poohed any idea that I was not being a good son, even when there were months between phone calls or visits. I could have done better.

I won't bother reminiscing about high school, other than to say I made a few great friends and (from my sophomore year on) did marginally well with the ladies, though I never quite got over a years-long infatuation with a girl named Pam Everhart. As has been a recurrent pattern in several of my relationships, a girl's family became more taken with me than the girl herself. Such was the case with Pam, who I suspect regarded me as no more than a good friend. But I pined away for a long time, even when dating other girls.

Getting older did not find me setting aside childish things so much as adding riskier ventures to them, like my first hesitant attempts at dating. What a curious, bewildering, inevitably embarrassing ritual. But the juices were flowing and, as Calvin of *Calvin and Hobbes* might say, I had no choice but to heed the call of the Y chromosome.

Otherwise, school was a bore, and I endured an undistinguished four years of crushing tedium and the customary adolescent chaos, albeit alleviated by a brief interlude in the limelight as a quasi-baritone singer in a folk music group called the Newcomers, joined by Steve Horton, Windon Blanton, Chris Baker and later Mont Hedrick. Chris, a fine guitarist, was the most talented. But Steve, my best and oldest childhood friend, is still at it in the 21st century, performing regularly in the Knoxville area, also having sired another generation of fine musicians. Steve was and remains a clever and gifted guy. Also a lucky one, having wed the smart and angelic Liz.

My weekend getaway was always to the neighboring town of Salisbury—by way of an unhealthy but seductive fried food emporium called the Chicken Shack—because Davidson County was dry, Rowan County was not, and I had developed a taste for beer. Bad beer as I learned years later—insipid, post-World War II watered-down lager like Pabst Blue Ribbon, Schlitz and

Budweiser. Ghastly stuff. But I knew no better at the time. It was also where I went to meet girls, though most of the time I struck out. "Let's just be friends" was a phrase I heard all too often.

But at least one of those female chums in Salisbury, Patsy Williams, introduced me to a bunch of her girlfriends, and every now and then something would come of it, especially later, when I was home from college.

My undistinguished high school career was topped off by an English teacher who refused to admit me to her writing class because she assayed my talent level and found it wanting. Based on my track record as a student she had every reason for doing so.

Not that I cared. School was not my thing at the time, anyway. Homework was something I did sporadically, and my classroom performance was not much better, to my parents' chagrin. I once complied with a chemistry teacher's instruction to "remove those electrons" from an atomic diagram by picking up an eraser and whisking them from the blackboard, not at all the method she had in mind. The class howled. So did the teacher. But I wasn't trying to be funny.

Still, it *is* funny how I am one of only two in our large senior class to make his or her living as a writer, and I've been at it twice as long as she was.

So there.

College Amid the '60s Youthquake

I can honestly say I never felt more alive than between 1968 and 1971, when the confluence of the ongoing civil rights movement, a rekindled ecological awareness, anti-Vietnam War protests, and a fervent push for female equality made for such a remarkable, and in some ways transformational, period of cultural and political ferment.

Today's conservatives would have us believe that the U.S. would have been infinitely better off had the naïve, monotone coma of the Eisenhower era not been questioned and held to scrutiny by the social and political groundswells of the 1960s and early 1970s. What a narrow vision. While it is true that the United States emerged from World War II as the most powerful nation in the world, power and virtue are not analogous. Yes, there was relief, and a measure of justifiable celebration, but the historically prosperous Eisenhower era also was characterized by stifling conformity, sexual repression, and a smug satisfaction with American exceptionalism. Not to mention an extraordinary amount of naïveté. A golden time—unless you happened to be Black, Asian, Native American, poor, or female.

Were there excesses in the movements, in the student uprisings of the time? Of course. What great, wrenching wave of perceptual change does not have pockets of extremism? But these do not invalidate what was pioneering, necessary, and useful in these movements. To dismiss these strides forward in a nation's maturation, to cite as preferable the self-satisfied, chauvinistic dogmas of the Reagan period, is to prefer a time when we Americans chose to believe again the most simplistic, feel-good myths about ourselves, to relinquish all skeptical faculties.

The Sixties woke us up. Some of us, at least. And the much-maligned Baby Boomers were in the vanguard. They owe no one an apology for giving a damn. I believe we compare quite favorably to the so-called "Greatest Generation," which has been decidedly overpraised for acquiescing to the norm. For all their admitted accomplishments, as a group they were the dominant standard-bearers of the conformist impulse.

For all of today's political rancor, for all the calcified partisanship and governmental ineptitude, for all the creeping cynicism, for all those who can't be bothered to vote, we are still better off because of what happened 50-odd years ago. No longer do we trust untrustworthy institutions. No longer do we endow "authority" with inviolate wisdom. No longer do we take things on faith or on face value. We care more for social justice, for racial amity, for the equality of women, and for a rapidly deteriorating environment. We are not the meek creatures of years past.

But let me climb down from my soap box, a most unseemly digression, and admit that it pains an old Lefty, here celebrating student activism of the 1960s and 70s, to reveal that he spent a year at a military prep school before making his way to college.

The less said of this interim year the better, though I will credit Carolina Military Academy in tiny Maxton, N.C., for teaching me how to study (there was nothing else to do but polish brass and boots and elude hazing). My first semester there as a post-high school grad was a too-radical change from the previous summer, a carefree romp spent largely at Ocean Drive Beach in South Carolina, drinking reservoirs of beer and chasing girls who had come down from the Midwest rather eager to meet a Southern boy. Shucks, we were happy to oblige.

The only respite from CMA's rigors and regimentation were the ample, leisurely breakfasts and sports—playing on the tennis team and traveling with the football and basketball squads as a stats geek. The rest of the time was spent in class, drilling, or dodging the teenage hard cases (some armed with knives and hair-trigger tempers) who had been exiled to military school because public schools couldn't handle them.

There was also the blessed relief of Saturday nights at the girls' school a few miles away in Red Springs. It was called Vardell Hall (gentlemanly restraint prevents me from revealing its nickname), and our bus trips to the realm of the feminine were met by stern-looking chaperones and alcohol-free punch at the socials. The multi-story women's dorm was distinguished by a rotunda from whose upper levels the girls who didn't have a date for the evening would gaze down to where you were seated, nervously waiting in a hot, uncomfortable wool dress uniform. No doubt they were sizing you up to see if you were worthy. It felt like being Daniel in the lionesses' den. Not an altogether unpleasant sensation, of course. Apart from being on stage, it's not often a guy has 20 or 30 young women looking at him speculatively, all at the same time.

The best thing about these escapes was being in the company of a bright and amiable southern belle named Anne Crutchfield, who was as lonely as me. One often wonders what became of the sweethearts of youth. I hope life has been a success for her.

Although my attitude has tempered a lot over the years, I have little positive to say about my direct brush with the military mind at that time, having the same objection to discipline for its own sake (however necessary) as I have to organized religion, which, to borrow a phrase from novelist John D. MacDonald, is like being marched in formation to go see a sunset.

Needless to say, 1967 was not my favorite year. I don't even remember what I did that summer when I secured my "release," beyond toiling at the typical summer job. In retrospect, it's amusing that a guy who never made it past buck private in military school would go on to interview Gen. William Westmoreland, Gen. Claudius Watts, Adm. Stanley Bump and Gen. James A. Grimsley and have each of them address me as "sir" when I strolled into their offices as a reporter.

I transferred to the University of North Carolina at Chapel Hill after two years (1968-69, 1969-70) at Wingate Junior College in tiny Wingate, N.C., gateway to the sybaritic pleasures of Charlotte. Halfway through my collegiate career, I was still not a good student. I would never have been admitted to UNC today with the grades I had at the time. But something changed, inexplicably, after I arrived in Chapel Hill. It was as if I went to bed one night as a relative slacker—far more interested in student activism and the great music of the day than academics—and woke up the next day fascinated with the learning process. I remain so to this day. And I have no idea what the pivot point was, or why. A cynic might suggest it was because I saw, consciously or unconsciously, the specter of the real working world just over the horizon and was prodded into seriousness. But, no, it just happened. My grades may not have always reflected this sudden devotion to my studies, but I was never at risk of flunking out, and what I was gaining was incalculable.

UNC's journalism school was rated among the best in the country in the 1970s, together with those of Stanford, Columbia University, Northwestern, and the University of Missouri. I was lucky to be there, but despite my academic sea change philosophically, I was a bit bedazzled during my first (junior) year, and it showed. At one point I was counseled by a newspaper editor-turned-professor that maybe journalism wasn't my calling. At the time, he had every reason for saying that, as I was relatively clueless about what journalism involved. I wonder what he would say if I saw him today. Probably I'd be congratulated but hear something like "At least you spared us by not going into *news*."

As Luck Would Have It

I am exceedingly grateful to all the professors at Wingate and UNC who made subjects come alive and fired my passion to know more, with a special shout out to a history professor, Charles Traynham, and an English prof, Harvey Lee Michael, both at Wingate, who were instrumental in my altered view of college and my decision-making as to a career. The former was the first teacher who really galvanized me. The latter rushed to my defense when I faced possible expulsion from Wingate, having dared to criticize the mystery meat being served in the cafeteria and worse, having written and disseminated an atheistic tract (it was a *Baptist* college).

I am also grateful to a professor of international relations at Davidson County Community College, where I picked up a couple of credits one summer. Having him as a professor was pure serendipity. He was a young fellow, not long removed from being a graduate assistant at Kent State University and a witness to the infamous National Guard massacre there. He made what might have been a dull subject fascinating. The great ones just have the *gift*. You didn't have to go to Harvard to have a great teacher.

Wingate was a place where I made a few life-long friends. Shared vicissitude, I suppose. One of my best pals was Bob Nunnenkamp, just as he is today. Apart from being a great guy, he never failed to set me up with a lovely blind date when we fled Wingate on weekends to visit his hometown of Charlotte. Come to think of it, he continued to set me up *after* college, too. And the Queen City had such cool nightclubs back in the day, joints like the Cove, Hornet's Nest Pub, the Drawbridge, the Cellar, the Purple Penguin and Jaguar. We prowled like cats.

Some of the lassies from that time—Bonnie Sharpe, Debbie Neal, Diane Dukelow, Joy Rice—I remember fondly. Thank you for your company.

But UNC was the place that got inside me, molded me. My experiences there affect me to this day. The timing was right to attend a great liberal arts university, one that fought its own battles for academic freedom against Far Right legislators—not least the execrable Jessie Helms—and all those who wished to silence dissident professors or the student body. UNC was also where I met my first love, Anne Dodson, the summer of my senior year. And a magical summer it was. (More on that later.) She was going to N.C. State over in the state capital, Raleigh, but to my good fortune she had decided to take some summer classes at UNC.

Chapel Hill was then and is now one of the most beautiful college campuses in America, and the town it inhabited was no less stimulating. I especially loved having outdoor classes, particularly in the amphitheater or arboretum. No longer was I gazing out a classroom window, daydreaming about being outside.

I lived in one of two high-rise dormitories called Granville Towers. One was strictly male students, the other female. But UNC, so liberal-minded a school that it was oft called the Berkeley of the East or Columbia of the South, then had a policy of 24-hour visitation between dorms. No chaperones, no guards, no nothing. Doubtless many a parent feared the towers represented Sodom and Gomorrah.

Though UNC and Duke University were and remain arch-rivals, the schools are only eight miles apart, and there was a lot of social interaction between their respective students. Many a warm afternoon would find UNC students lolling about in the sylvan splendor of Duke Gardens or admiring that campus's striking, if rather dour, Gothic architecture.

When I was back home visiting the folks, I'd often pal around with an old high school chum, Eddie Wike, who I got to know far better after we'd graduated from high school. We spent many an evening in the cool confines of the Rathskeller in Salisbury, quaffing brews and chewing over current events. During summers, we often took a road trip.

Unfortunately, I have not retained many friends from my collegiate years—I'm not altogether sure why—but those I have are special to me, like Bob Nunnenkamp and Howard Platt. Like me, Howie started his journalism career in sports, but stuck with the field far longer than I, in his case as a broadcaster. Bob, who also transferred to Chapel Hill before going to UNC-Charlotte, wound up being a highly successful Pepsi Cola executive.

Compared to where I'd grown up, Chapel Hill was culture with a capital "C." In addition to all the fine local musicians, great international musical

As Luck Would Have It

acts of the day would come to Chapel Hill, especially during a three-day spring event called Jubilee. Among those who played that gig while I was in school—and all of whom I saw—were James Taylor (whose dad was chief orthopedic surgeon at UNC Medical Center), Smokey Robinson, Joe Cocker, Tina Turner, B.B. King, Chuck Berry, Leon Russell, the Allman Brothers, Richie Havens, Carole King, John Sebastian, Grand Funk Railroad, Spirit, Muddy Waters, the J. Geils Band, Tom Rush, Chicago, the Paul Butterfield Blues Band, Ten Wheel Drive, and Earth, Wind & Fire, among others. Janis Joplin was to have appeared as well, but died before she could make the scene. I wish I remember more about the concerts, but many of us were in an "altered state of consciousness" some of the time.

I saw the Allman Brothers for the first time during the July 16-18, 1970 run of the extraordinary Love Valley Rock Festival, also known as "Woodstock South." Anne and I had driven up not knowing what we would find, and were stunned. Held on the outskirts of a mock-Old West town of the same name in the North Carolina mountains, it drew between 60,000 and 200,000 young people, depending on whose estimates one believed, all wanting to share in Woodstock's afterglow. The various bands played from the early afternoons deep into the nights, with steep mountainside seating sporting a sea of blankets and lit candles, like a million fireflies pulsing. Between sets, what seemed like a million crickets chimed in from the surrounding forest with their own wafting symphony, and this magical sound broke over us like waves on a beach.

The Allman Brothers had just one album out at the time, and were largely unknown, a status that soon would be remedied. But we were transfixed. Copious amounts of wine and marijuana might have had something to do with it, a counteragent to the mysterious gruel served up by a number of "soup kitchens" at the festival. There was even a small contingent of Hell's Angels types there to provide unofficial security. In any case, peace reigned from start to finish.

The summer of my senior year was golden. I owned my first car, a used 1966 Mustang 289 convertible, resplendent in medium blue with white interior and propelled by a frisky V8. I never got to find out if it was a "chick magnet" (as advertised) because the first girl I met that summer made sure she was the last one I'd meet for a while. A week after we met, Anne Dodson and I were inseparable, but we were hardly insular. Anne had the natural ability to turn strangers into friends in short order, where I was not quite as outgoing. I recall one afternoon when I slipped away from a park where we were taking our ease to buy a couple of Cokes, only to return to where I'd left her, sitting under a tree and playing her guitar—for 12 people who hadn't been there 10 minutes earlier.

Still one of the most romantic moments in my life was with her, lying on a blanket in the quiet of the campus arboretum at night, kissing softly as a gentle rain fell down. Right out of the movies.

In between spring and fall semesters at these various schools, my parents made certain I didn't dawdle away my vacation but rather took on a variety of summer jobs. They ranged from nasty to horrid to arduous, though some had features of interest. I readily discovered what I did *not* want to do with the rest of my life. The motivation to finish college was correspondingly high. This, no doubt, was my parents' aim all along, for me to experience how others lived and be grateful for my advantages. It gave me a keen appreciation of, and respect for, so many necessary but unenviable and even soul-killing tasks in which people spent their entire lives.

When I did graduate from college, unlike high school, I was sure of it before standing backstage in a cap and gown hoping my name was going to be called. I do regret playing the disdainful hippie card and denying my folks a chance to see me walk across the stage as a UNC graduate, especially after they had worked so hard to get me there. I was too contemptuous of the "hollowness" of traditional ritual, and just had the university mail the diploma to me. Fittingly, the parchment crinkled up badly when framed. Karma, I suppose.

Bring on the Working World, or Becoming a Writer

The year was 1971, and my confidence was in short supply. I was sitting at the desk in my old bedroom (before Mom remodeled my personal history away), trying to write a sample story of a game I'd just watched on TV, as required by prospective employers. It was a first attempt. Having no experience beyond a modest talent for bullshitting in college and wondering how in the devil I was ever going to do it, I trudged away.

Despite the encouragement of my mom and girlfriend, Anne, with whom I was soon to cohabit, privately I was asking myself whatever possessed me to think I could write.

After visiting several papers who took a tentative bite at my lure, the job offer came from the *Daily Press* of Newport News, Va., an entry-level newspaper of the sort we in the trade used to call a "rabbit farm," a place where unproven talent could break in and see if they could cut the mustard. Though I had grown up in North Carolina less than 300 miles away, I had never heard of the city, nor its companion community, Hampton.

But the Tidewater area, as southeastern Virginia is called, is well-situated: Only an hour from Richmond or Virginia Beach, two hours from the Shenandoah Valley or Washington, D.C., and three from Baltimore. Nearby cities and towns like Williamsburg, Norfolk, Portsmouth, Chesapeake and Yorktown all had things to commend them to visitors, though I don't think I fully appreciated that at the time.

The *Daily Press* offered me my choice of two jobs. Newport News, like Norfolk, was a big military town, with Air Force and Army bases. They were looking for a reporter who would focus on the latter, Fort Eustis (which some unnamed wag had dubbed "Even Uncle Sam Thinks It Stinks").

The paper also needed a sportswriter. Given the fact that I was just out of college with long hair and an antipathy toward everything militaristic, my choice was a no-brainer. But it was more than wanting nothing to do with the military. Unlike newswriting and the straitjacket of terse Associated Press style, sportswriting gave its practitioners the freedom to write with gusto and wit, to let it rip like a Curry Kirkpatrick, then an audacious scribe for *Sports Illustrated,* and a personal hero.

Even though I had once imagined myself to be a journalistic crusader-in-the-making, destined to help change the world through brilliant news reporting, the fact was that too many news writers got stuck covering dreary, crushingly dull subjects, no matter how vital to the public good. By contrast, the world of sports was a grand *spectacle*: alive, vigorous, fun. The strength, talent, and fortitude one saw on the playing fields and courts were real, not some movie hero gunning down collapsing extras.

So, it was a done deal. Accompanied by Anne, and with a small U-Haul trailer in tow, I drove my beloved 1966 Mustang convertible north by northeast to a new life.

I had the first job jitters, just a little bit daunted. But the sports room was busy, convivial, and comradely in the main, filled with eccentric characters and directed by one Charles Karmosky, still the most organized, best prepared department editor with whom I have ever worked. And a bit of a dragon, too.

He was one hard-nosed hombre when he wished to be. But like many tough guys, he could betray a soft center. He ran a department with an unusually large number of full-time reporters, layout artists and copy editors, especially for a mid-size daily newspaper. He was also the most powerful man in the newsroom. Senior news editors, accustomed to looking down on sports and feature writers, might come at him like lions, but they left like lambs.

As Luck Would Have It

I cut my teeth on the usual cub reporter assignments, keeping my head down and saying "Yes, sir" a lot. In other words, not expecting a summons from *The New York Times* or *Sports Illustrated* anytime soon.

So how unexpected it was, little more than a year later, when the *Daily Press* handed me the plum of all plums: the National Football League beat. No one was more surprised than I was at being entrusted with it, and it must have created some resentment on the part of a few of the veteran staffers who might have coveted the job. But nobody ever said anything. I suppose the attitude was "Give the rookie a chance."

And what a contrast to the rudimentary tasks of covering Little League, high school, American Legion, and small college games, or the daily chore of sorting wire service copy for the Desk.

I still sported shoulder-length hair from my recent hippie past—a political statement, not a fashion one—and although my girlfriend liked the long locks, my dad had cautioned me that it was time to shear them as well as to wear grown-up clothes. After all, he reasoned, I'd be sharing a press box with sophisticated, and perhaps judgmental, journalistic swells. Not so, as it turned out. No one cared about my hair, and I dressed acceptably enough in old tweeds and corduroy jeans. Compared to the sea of leisure suits and tobacco-stained T-shirts I was seeing, I presented a bohemian polish.

Being the beat man covering the then-Washington Redskins and Baltimore Colts meant traveling to and exploring exciting major cities I'd never seen and immersing myself in them. And they were paying me to do it!

Plus, getting to watch and interview many a youthful hero up close. I didn't even mind the cold hot dogs and warm cokes served the press in D.C., because other cities and other franchises feted you royally—perhaps too royally. This was before editors, stung by accusations of petty graft and influence peddling, called an abrupt halt to all freebies a writer could accept at the stadium. Goodbye crab cakes and Crêpes Suzette, au revoir lobster Newberg and shrimp Creole. Adios Danish pastries and fresh soft pretzels and steaming burgers with all the trimmings. Hello, spartan dining. Or worse, McDonald's.

Bill Thompson

As my newspaper had been covering the Redskins and Colts just about as long as had the *Washington Post* and *Baltimore* Sun—and longevity was accorded deference—I found myself seated in a rarefied position between the *Post* and Associated Press reporters. This, on the *front* row (45-yard line) of the press box at old RFK Stadium and with almost as desirable a seat at the late, lamented Memorial Stadium in Baltimore.

This was tall cotton. I was a callow 23, suddenly thrust into the Bigs (albeit not for a Big League newspaper) and in the company of legends. Not just the great athletes but the renowned sportswriters, above all the *Post's* natty, faintly aristocratic Shirley Povich. Somehow, the confidence I'd been lacking years earlier was now, magically, my best friend. Where it came from I do not know. I hadn't had enough experience for that to be the source. I was not cowed by my setting or my more seasoned colleagues. What was intimidating were multiple deadlines, a crappy portable typewriter, and a blank sheet of paper. Yet the words tumbled out anyway, to my astonishment.

In Baltimore, reporters were also allowed to leave the press box in the fourth quarter if they wished, go down to the field and walk the sidelines. Who could say no to that? The sounds of huge bodies crashing into each other with malicious intent is quite a different sensation down in the nitty-gritty than it is up in the stands. The violence of the sport is vividly, wincingly real. But seeing a great running back or fleet receiver dashing by you a few feet away *en route* to a touchdown was a singular experience.

The NFL beat also came with luxuries like Western Union. During the three and a half years I covered the league, most teams not only supplied you with halftime and post-game statistics, but positioned the Western Union typists close by. Exclusively women, they were supernaturally brisk at the keyboard, transcribing and transmitting error-free versions of your story to your newspaper's offices as you finished each page and handed it to a runner to deliver to them. This was particularly valuable during a Monday Night Game, when, because of its late-night duration, you had to file a halftime story as well as a final one. I'll always be grateful to the typists and the runners.

As Luck Would Have It

Contrast this with covering many small college sports on the road, often forced to stand in a rural phone booth in a driving rain, balancing a balky telecopier on your knee only to have an operator unfamiliar with the machine's squeal cut you off mid transmission—with 10 minutes to go before deadline. Or being forced to "write" the story off the top of your head, in that same drafty phone booth, summer or winter, dictating it to another reporter down the line. Or trying to write a basketball story on the press row of a converted aircraft hangar—the "arena" for some schools—with a college's brass band blaring away one row behind you.

Of course, there were downsides even to the NFL beat. While I flew to other cities to cover games when either the Redskins or Colts were on the road, I drove to D.C. and Baltimore when the teams were home. No problem in crisp fall weather. But the press box at RFK was open air, which meant arctic conditions in the dead of winter, with a nasty wind whipping at you from the first moment of the game until the last. And since we wrote our game stories from our positions after returning from locker room interviews, front-row reporters found themselves chattering as fiercely as the typewriter. Ever tried to type with gloves on frozen fingers? Problematic.

Stadium parking was either privileged or perilous. The *Daily Press* was the city's morning paper, the *Times-Herald* its evening counterpart. I had to share an RFK Stadium parking pass with my opposite number on the evening paper, a senior staffer also covering the Redskins. He would get it one year, me the next, which meant one of us parked a few feet from the stadium entrance and the other was banished two hundred yards closer to the Potomac. It was no fun leaving the stadium at 1:30 a.m. after a Monday Night Game, walking through that dark and shadowed parking lot where muggings were known to happen. I was always carrying a valise and a typewriter back to the car, and I kept them swinging and at the ready.

Then there was driving home to Virginia in a snowstorm, which I did all too often, once from Baltimore in a company car with bald tires and fitful windshield wipers, and on icy roadways not yet cleared. Nine hours to make a three-hour drive. Sportswriters deal with crazy weather routinely. I have plenty of horror stories in my Journalist's Book of Miseries. Stay tuned.

Lest I get a big head from covering the Big Leagues, my time in Virginia also involved covering small-college sports, which helped keep my feet on the ground. And in most cases, the athletes that gave their all weren't doing it with a realistic eye toward going to the pros, but simply out of love for the game. That was refreshing. I had attended a fairly large university where basketball was tantamount to religion, and everyone took it very seriously indeed.

There was also the tranquil pastoral quality of many small-college stadiums as opposed to their university or big city counterparts. The backdrops could be beautiful. Washington and Lee in Lexington, Va., springs immediately to mind. Going to a game there was like attending a garden party with blankets spread on grassy knolls with a couple of thousand breezy, lazy celebrants instead of the hysteria of 60,000 fans living and dying on the outcome.

Across town it was a very different matter, with the setting of Virginia Military Institute most resembling a gulag. Curious, considering that other military academies—The Citadel, West Point, Annapolis, the Air Force Academy, and Coast Guard Academy—all rest in notably lovely surrounds.

Though one wrote stories about the pro and college football teams throughout the year, when the gridiron season ended, I'd return to basketball, baseball, tennis and so on, more or less full-time (soccer hadn't made many inroads in the early '70s). I have many happy memories of those days, not least being a reporter covering Roanoke College and Old Dominion University when they won national small college championships.

At one time I also was a basketball beat writer covering Christopher Newport College and, across the way in Norfolk, Hampton Institute (a.k.a, the Black Harvard). I'll never forget the first game I covered at Hampton, being just about the only white guy in a 7,000-seat arena, and thinking nothing of it, apart from feeling welcomed.

As Luck Would Have It

Although I did not cover the Atlantic Coast Conference, long the mecca of college basketball, I did wind up covering one of the great events in the history of American sports. When our usual ACC beat man was hurt in a minor car wreck, the assignment of covering the NCAA Championship Semifinals and Finals was offered to me. What made it momentous was that the semis was a showdown between the No. 1 and No. 2-ranked teams in the land, North Carolina State and David Thompson against Bill Walton and mighty UCLA. The latter, under coaching great John Wooden, had won seven NCAA titles in a row.

What made it especially sweet was that the Final Four was being played for the first time in my home state—Greensboro, N.C., to be precise—and that I was a life-long N.C. State fan. Wearing a mask of journalistic impartiality on Press Row no was mean feat. But I managed it.

It was a game of the ages. N.C. State won, 80-77, in double overtime. Memorable, to say the least.

I also had enough memories of covering the Redskins and Colts—from the exciting to the bizarre—to last me a couple of lifetimes. Aside from many a memorable game, there were the odd incidents, such as small aircraft buzzing stadiums to a heavy fog rolling in and totally obscuring the playing field, for fans and players alike, during a game's final moments.

When not working, Anne and I often could be found hanging with friends north of Richmond at Randolph-Macon College, inner-tubing down the nearby North Anna River, going to concerts at Tidewater-area coliseums or haunting the clubs at Virginia Beach. Our timing could not have been better in that last regard. The music scene in Virginia Beach in the early 1970s was amazing, with scores of top-notch area bands. One in particular captured our imagination and won our loyalty, a trio of troubadours named Larson, House and Jones (a.k.a., Coyote, Robby and Mike). To this day, I've never heard better. Seriously.

Occasionally we'd range farther out. Like Richmond's funky old district called "The Fan," then a hippie enclave. Norfolk likewise had an older sector of the city called Ghent, and both had a well-established, vibrant music scene. But few venues could top Norfolk's acoustically and architecturally impressive Chrysler Hall.

At one point I made the grievous mistake of trading in Abigail, my classic Mustang—not knowing it was about to become a classic—for Angela, a Mercury Capri in British racing green. In this little green hornet Anne and made our first trip out of the country. Well, mine anyway. It was to Montreal. All along the way, when not taking in the scenery, we continued to speak to each other in "Pandamonium," our silly but endearing personal argot of affection we'd devised in college. We pretended we were panda bears in another life, reincarnated as humans. Give us a break; we were smitten with each other, and still just kids.

Montreal was a blast. It would be quite some time before I had the money to enjoy foreign travel again.

Back to work. I had my successes at the *Daily Press*. But one's professional gaffes tend to linger longer in the mind and are, in retrospect, often quite amusing. I had some doozies. In those days, every newspaper had an editor who kept a scrapbook of hilarious blunders and wild typos that, embarrassingly, made their way into print. Mine should have made the scrapbook's front page.

One stands out. In 1974, a Who's Who of professional basketball stars from the established NBA and upstart ABA played a charity All-Star game at the Richmond Coliseum, and I was there to cover it. Proceeds were to go to an organization doing research about heroin addiction. Commenting on the big crowd that had shown up to see the stars, and what that meant in terms of gate receipts, the third paragraph of my game story read "The program got a well-deserved shot in the arm."

What I'd written didn't hit me until I was halfway back to Newport News, far too late to call the sports department and get them to make a hasty change in my copy. But to my amazement, no one caught it, in or out of the newsroom. No one called, irate over my unconscionably poor taste. No letters demanding I be censured or fired.

I made a number of good friends in Virginia. A few of these relationships have lasted to this day. I only wish I could see these chums more often. Colleagues and confidantes like Mike Keech, Joe Fudge (a former roomie), Alan Kovski, Marianne Pastor, Mike Morgan and Peggy Crowder (couple with whom I spent countless hours), and Craig Nuckles stand out. Until a recent (2021), regrettable and apparently irreparable falling out, Kovski was one of my three closest friends, a hiking buddy, correspondent, and intellectual companion par excellence. It saddens me every time I think about it.

I miss the people I haven't seen in a long while.

After 18 months of living together, Anne and I drifted apart. It was not so much that our ardor or regard for each other had cooled, but that external factors (which I am not at liberty to divulge) had compelled us to call it a day. Both of us were saddened. You never quite get over that first genuine love affair.

I had a few other girlfriends after Anne and I broke up, most memorably a wild-child Ohioan named Brenda Lee Lomax, but whom everyone called "Sunshine." And what a trip *she* was. Petite, smart but mercurial, and sexy as hell.

But Anne remained—and remains—my fondest memory of college and my first year in Virginia.

I would only see her one more time, years later in Charleston, S.C. She had come there from Houston with her new husband and daughter to have an operation. After that brief visit, we lost touch. To this day, I wonder what became of my first love. I tried to find out, off and on, over the course of a few years, if only to know she was all right. But I never could track her down.

After a dry spell (I've had more than my share, romantically), into the gap flew the prettiest (and chattiest) girl I ever called my own, Chris Davenport. She was a military brat, the daughter of a retired Navy captain and an Australian mom who had come to Virginia after living in Hawaii and San Diego. Chris was a young divorcee and mother ready to reenter the dating world. I was more than happy to oblige. And I was quite taken with her two-year-old daughter, Kirsten. Like me, Chris loved movies and concerts, and we went to a bunch, with performances by Joni Mitchell and Bonnie Raitt being particularly delightful memories.

I wish I could remember more of the people and events from the Virginia years. There are many faces and places that flit in and out of memory's eye now, tantalizingly close to recognition before fading away. But sometimes they resolve, and in that moment I am warmed.

One memory that remains indelible was salt and freshwater fishing with Mike Morgan, which we did at every opportunity, frequently stoned on grass. It enhanced the drama of angling.

I very much enjoyed my years at the *Daily Press* and living in Virginia. I learned that entertaining people could be almost as important as informing them, and that keen observation and a dollop of flair were prime conduits for doing so. But like many young journalists, there came a time (1976) when I was ready to move on to other places, other challenges, and (marginally) bigger paychecks.

Enter the siren song of Florida, complete with palm trees and alligators. Colleagues threw me a happy/sad farewell party. I said a tentative goodbye to Chris and was off. What I didn't predict was that Chris and Kirsten would soon follow me south.

Way Up North (in Florida)

Jacksonville was something of a surprise after almost five years in the Old Dominion.

It wasn't that Jacksonville was that much bigger a city, population-wise, than the Newport News/Hampton twin towns. Jax (as the locals call it) was nothing like a metropolis until it was consolidated with all of Duval County in 1968. Overnight, it was a physical approximation of a major city, rivalling Los Angeles in land area.

Despite the palm tree trappings, the sensibility of the city was more South Georgia than North Florida, and the glowing, vibrant looking cityscape at night—festooned with insurance company towers—was revealed to be a charade. Downtown closed the sidewalks at 5 p.m., and the action, such as it was, was in the burbs or at the beach. While there was a local symphony orchestra and other pleasures, the cultural ambiance of the time consisted largely of garage bands imitating Lynyrd Skynyrd. Many of the refinements I'd taken for granted in Virginia did not yet exist here, including at the newspaper, which was still using cut-and-paste methods years after I'd switched from ancient 1940s typewriters to computers in Virginia.

Thinking I had left the "hinterlands" of Virginia to enjoy the upscale delights of Florida, I had rematerialized in something altogether less. I had thought Virginia behind the times, but it was positively cosmopolitan compared to Jacksonville, at least in 1976. I was still a sportswriter, but unlike the 10,000-seat coliseums and arenas to which I'd grown accustomed in Virginia, there were more dinky aircraft hangars, even at major universities. Of course, the football stadiums were huge, and Jax had the Gator Bowl. Still, I was a bit dismayed, though pleased with a superior newsroom and the picturesque riverside restaurant the newspaper offered employees.

I also enjoyed moonlighting as a writer on contemporary music, which I did for the paper's rather threadbare in-house magazine, *Changes*. Because the dominant pop music form of the day was Disco, which I thought vapid and cordially disliked, I turned to older standbys like Bob Dylan and the Rolling Stones. I also began, in earnest, a lifelong relationship with jazz.

I covered one last NFL game, this time featuring the Tampa Bay Buccaneers, and handled various other assignments before getting the University of Georgia football beat. This was during the highly successful Vince Dooley era, and Georgia was just as big a deal to Jacksonville readers as the University of Florida in Gainesville or Florida State in Tallahassee. The University of Miami had yet to become a national power.

I always got a kick out of driving up to Sanford Stadium in Athens, barreling down the backroads through all the small Victorian towns along the way, covering the occasional prep game in towns like Waycross, Valdosta, and Thomasville, where high school football was almost a religion.

If high school sports represented a "come down" from covering the pros, I did not mind so much. The fact is, I was never all that ambitious in terms of my career. As with so many other things in my life—romantic relationships, life in general—I just let things happen. Things just fall into your lap from time to time, and to a certain extent my life has been a case study in the phenomenon. I'm not especially proud of this laissez-faire attitude, but neither was I completely passive about my path. I've never been a goal-setter in the strict sense (I find it artificial), but when the situation called for it, I would make my move.

Anyway, as the fabled runner from Marathon must have said, "Back to Athens."

The picturesque stadium "between the hedges" reminded me of UNC's Keenan Stadium, surrounded by a pastoral backdrop of tall trees. But Georgia Bulldogs fans took their football far more seriously than did the Tar Heels, for whom football was just something one did to kill time before the onset of basketball season.

Football season in Jacksonville was dominated by two key events: the annual Gator Bowl, played in the 60,000-seat stadium of the same name, and the yearly Florida-Florida State game, famously known (then and now) as the "World's Largest Outdoor Cocktail Party."

I also was beat writer for Jacksonville University basketball program, just a few years following its one and only trip to the NCAA Finals with its All-America center Artis Gilmore. JU never again attained such a lofty position.

The *Florida Times-Union* sports staff, first under the leadership of Maynard Eilers, and later of David Lamm during my years there, was a diverse bunch, generally less eccentric (and thus less interesting) than some of the staffers with whom I'd worked in Newport News, but seasoned and capable.

Like most newshounds, we spun yarns of Herculean feats and bizarre incidents with each other. Some were even true, like the shared experience of five or six of us with a different sort of canine at the Orange Park Greyhound Track. Jai alai might have been the main attraction for gamblers in south Florida, but here it was greyhounds. There was a dog racing circuit in Florida back then, and the tracks were minor palaces, with outstanding restaurants. I had little interest in gambling, but sampling Beef Wellington and the great 1950s-style desert classics like Cherries Jubilee and Peach Melba were a different matter.

The word was that the dog tracks in the state were Mob owned, and racing was a huge source of gambling revenue for track owners and, one assumed, the state. Certain things that happened when the track managers tried to "fete" us reporters gave a certain credence to the organized crime suspicion. I recall my first Christmas at the *Times-Union*, when I arrived at my desk one day to see a nondescript envelope addressed to me. I opened it to find two $100 bills. I noticed that every other desk had one, too.

So I asked Maynard, "What gives?" He said, "Oh, that. Don't worry about it. It's like a game. They send them to us each year as a Christmas gift, and the reporters mail them back. Obviously, you can't keep it."

Some decided they would just go to the track, bet on a long shot and lose it all back. That worked fine until one of our number won a trifecta and turned his $200 into $1,500. He had to spend three days intentionally losing it.

I didn't want the money (though I certainly could have used 200 bucks). But it always puzzled me. The track manager's gesture had to be more in the way of public relations—currying favor or goodwill rather than overt graft; just the way they operated—because no one in the sports department actually covered dog racing or gambling. All we ever did was run daily race results in tiny agate type—the racing equivalent of baseball box scores, or horse show results. No articles, no profiles, like we would for other sports. Yet for several years, like clockwork, the envelopes arrived. And were returned.

But it was cool to be able to go down into the kennels now and then to meet the dogs and their handlers. A decade or so later I learned that the conditions of the track's kennels and the supreme health of the dogs were the anomaly, and that the greyhounds who didn't make the cut as racing dogs were treated cruelly. It was a scandal that finally came to light and forced considerable change.

As Luck Would Have It

Our HQ enjoyed a picturesque location at No. 1 Riverside Avenue, overlooking the St. John's River. The building also was close to some of my favorite old neighborhoods like Riverside and Avondale, as well as a small but piquant hub of commercial and cultural activity called, inevitably, Five Points. When I wasn't on the road, the newsroom was home, and a typical workday there consisted of doing a couple of phone interviews, knocking out a few stories, and then enduring hours of crushing boredom punctuated—especially on Saturday nights—with spasms of lunatic frenzy.

My first three years in newspapering in Virginia had found me pounding away on 1940s-vintage typewriters, following a cut-and-paste approach to copy, with typesetting done in the back shop with venerable old linotype machines and their highly skilled operators, who had to read upside-down to set lead type. The process was what they used to call "hot type." Suddenly, that was steam-age stuff. The *Daily Press* had entered the modern world with electronic typewriters, then—glory be—with computers!

Little did I suspect that, like other facets of a culture lost in time, the Jacksonville paper was still doing cut-and-paste when I arrived there. It was *another* year before we got computers and I was in the weird position of being asked (unofficially) to teach.

(Parenthetically, guess what happened when I moved to Charleston in 1980? Yep, you guessed it. Cut-and-paste. And when they got computers a year or so later, I was teaching again.)

But back to Jax.

I had been in North Florida for about four months when Chris and I agreed that she and Kirsten would join me. They arrived at my tiny little apartment, with its pitiful double bed, apparently happy to be in a new environment. But I knew we would need a larger apartment; we couldn't shuffle Kirsten from the lone bed to the couch forever.

Meanwhile, I had made the fortuitous acquaintance of a young security guard there, a bespectacled redheaded fellow named Bill Petry, who would evolve into one of my closest friends until his death in 2011.

Bill Thompson

Bill was an auto-didact, a voluminous reader on many subjects, his erudition and range of interests beggared that of many college graduates. From literature to the natural world, movies to radio to music and beyond, I probably learned more from him than anyone I've ever met. I also smoked more grass with him than anyone else, too. And we had our share of adventures. Our chief haunts were amid the dunes of the then almost primordial Ponte Vedra Beach (now overrun with development), and a place simply called the Monument, actually part of the Fort Caroline National Monument and maybe the only spot of high ground in the state.

Sitting atop St. John's Bluff and affording a gorgeous bird's eye view of the river and its shipping lanes, the crest had a small sitting area featuring a low, curved stone wall, a stone bench, and the sentinel of a broad, gnarled oak tree, like something out of a H.P. Lovecraft or Washington Irving story. We'd sit there at night, usually accompanied by our girlfriends, playing guitar, smoking weed, and savoring the vistas.

But the parking area below was so infamous as a lover's lane that when the surrounding acreage known as Monument Park became an official state park, free 24-hour access was stopped by a locked gate. End of an era. Today it's part of the expansive Timucuan Preserve National Park.

Another favorite getaway for Bill, Chris and me was St. Augustine, down A1A from the Jax beaches. The old tourist part of town was entertaining enough, but the prize at its edge was the Milltop, a ramshackle bar and music venue with a splendid second-story, tree-shaded deck. Warm weather afternoons and nights there could not be beat. One of my favorite joints ever.

St. Augustine was also where I met an exceptional artist named Duke Kilgore, some of whose hand-carved wood sculptures still fill my home and draw the admiring eye of visitors. He fashioned brilliant, usually minimalist statues and reliefs of the human figure from blocks of exotic woods like Mozambique teak. He never used a power tool, and his approach was much like that of Rodin, who once remarked "The work of art is already within the block of marble. I just chop off whatever isn't needed." Duke was also a skilled and published cartooned. Though I saw him infrequently, I became quite friendly with him and his wife Sherry.

But I digress again.

Curiosity and creativity ran in Bill's family. He was the second oldest of six children, all of whom were talented in one way or another. Much like their father. Bill Senior earned degrees in chemistry and bacteriology at St. Louis University before beginning a 30-year career as a brewer. Shortly after retiring from Anheuser-Busch, he moved his family to Jacksonville. He worked at the local electric company but really came alive as an actor in community theater.

Meanwhile, Bill Sr.'s home workshop turned out everything from canoes and furniture to small working aircraft. Not to mention the wonderful handmade Christmas gifts he produced for each of his children every year. He also had a penchant for making and burying (to his family's relief) a particularly lethal version of Korean kimchi. When Bill Sr. decided the time was right to unearth it, the kids fled to other tables at other venues.

The matriarch of the clan, Joanne, a cross between June Cleaver and Liv Ullman, staunch and steadfast. She adopted me into the family. And I never really left. I even dated Bill's younger sister, Lisa, for a while.

Bill Jr. possessed some of the same aptitudes as his father, but he wasn't really suited for school. His problem in adulthood was that he was almost always a great deal more intelligent and capable than those he worked for, and it grated on him. Bill worked as a line cook, a fast-food restaurant manager, and a cab driver/dispatcher, among other jobs. He would have been a superb park ranger given the chance, but could not meet the educational requirements. I often wondered what might have been. He had the gifts to do so much more. Much like me, his chief ambitions were to be useful, to learn, and to enjoy life. Sadly, he suffered bouts of depression in later years, and it proved his undoing. But he was a kind, humorous, and loving man, and I miss him. Forty-four years on, I am still close to his widow, Cindy. She and I talk family and baseball in the main, but we've sustained our connection. How I look forward to her Christmas cookies!

Bill Thompson

It was due to Bill that I met Karyl Lee, an artist and purveyor of fine fabrics who eventually moved to Charleston, S.C. to go to the culinary college Johnson & Wales. She stayed on to be a caterer and credible health food guru in addition to her art. We resumed our friendship when she arrived, often cooking together. Ours was a special relationship until her death a few years ago in Ohio, where she had moved to care for elderly relatives.

Cohabiting with Chris and Kirsten went swimmingly for about three years, with a major upgrade of apartments closer to one of the Jacksonville area's numerous beaches. Our apartment complex, University Lakes, also had the added bonus of being directly behind the Alhambra Dinner Theater, one of the nation's most successful for many years.

One may disparage dinner theater and summer stock as places where perpetual unknowns and stars on the downslope of their careers go to act, but the Alhambra showcased solid talents, not least the bouncy, effervescent Robert Morse. After a brief flash of stardom in Hollywood reprising his stage role in "How to Succeed in Business Without Really Trying" in the early '60s, his career faltered. A decade later, he appeared at the Alhambra in the lead of Woody Allen's "Play It Again, Sam" with a *Playboy* Playmate of the Year as a co-star, and one might have assumed his career was nearing an end.

But it wasn't all that long before Morse had a triumphant return to Broadway, winning his second Tony Award for his performance as Truman Capote in "Tru." He'd add a Screen Actor's Guild Award to his mantle later. Lives in the arts *can* have a second act, or more.

Kirsten sailed through the terrible twos and threes with nary a ripple, though Chris and I, like most couples, had our differences and ups and downs. Eventually we parted, on good terms. She lives in Australia these days, and we're still good friends.

For a time, I dated a very attractive young Iranian-American lady named Shirin Firouzabadian, whose family had had to flee the revolution of fundamentalist Islamic clerics led by the Ayatollah Khomeini in 1979. Thoroughly modern and "Americanized," Shirin liked the United States.

But she longed to return home and resume her career teaching English and fighting for women's rights.

It was Chris, always the matchmaker, who introduced me to my last girlfriend in Florida, Anna Lia Pialorsi, a lithe, compact dancer only a generation removed from Italy, and with the culinary chops to prove it. We were a romantic item during what I call The Interregnum, that year in the desert after leaving the *Times-Union* (sort of a mutual decision between myself and the paper) and my landing a real job in South Carolina.

That interim year in the Wilderness, was spent doing jobs for which I had no real capacity, like sales. Meanwhile, I was getting my feet wet at free-lance writing, with half-hearted effort and minimal success. I quickly learned I'd not inherited my dad's gift for sales, be it of water conditioners, freezers, engine additives or anything else. I had the journalist's need to impart as much information as possible, well after I'd made the sale—only to lose it. Like those summer jobs I had during college, I discovered what I did not want to do with the rest of my life. At least I got to knock around with fellow sales agent Nita Donivan, one of the most intriguing and beautiful women I've ever met. This, of course, was before Ms. Pialorsi appeared, cutting board in hand.

My culinary education really began in Florida. The dog racing track at Orange Park contained one of my favorite restaurants, along with Dane's in Five Points (and its marvelous Chicken Kiev), and, farther afield, Strickland's. Hard by the St. John's ferry, it was the jewel of Mayport, a fishing village that is one of the oldest incorporated burgs in Florida. The commercial fishing boats docked next door, and the entrance to the restaurant went through a fish monger's station, where you could choose your meal from the finfish and shellfish that had been lain on ice less than an hour before. Superb, especially the grouper, red snapper, pompano, and the restaurant's signature mullet (yes, mullet) dip, a rare delicacy from a fish that other regions dismissed as bait.

In May of 1980, I said *arrivederci* to Anna Lia (though I would drive back to visit over the next few months, as we had not officially broken up) and departed for Charleston. Happily, it wasn't long before she met someone else.

I would return to visit the Petrys on many occasions, but I was ready to trade one coastal city for another.

Doing the Charleston (First Dance)

I was 32 when I arrived in the Holy City, as it is called, to work for the oldest daily newspaper in the South, the *News and Courier*. And it was a culture shock. Both the paper and the city.

Many locals still seemed to be fighting the Civil War—the "Late Unpleasantness" was a tongue-in-cheek tag preferred by some wags, alternate euphemisms by others. Maintaining a sense of history is valuable, obsessing over a "Lost Cause" that no one should revere is a different matter entirely. Though my maternal grandmother had been a card-carrying member of the Daughters of the Confederacy, she was equally devoted to the Daughters of the American Revolution. She had a part-time Black maid, Lizzie, for many years, and to us grandkids she was simply a member of our family. Though I suspect the feeling was not entirely mutual.

What my grandmother suggested, my mom made plain: Slavery was wrong and shameful, a tragedy. In any place, in any era.

Charleston had been the very seat of the Western Hemispheric slave trade, though today we know that the North wasn't exactly slave-free, either, nor did many a Northern profiteer disdain the trade altogether.

In her excellent *Sojourns in Charleston, 1865-1947* (University of South Carolina Press, 2019), Jennie Holton Fant recounts the story of the De Wolfe family of Rhode Island as unearthed by a descendant, filmmaker Katrina Browne. Browne revealed that her most prominent ancestor, James De Wolfe (1764-1837), a U.S. Senator and merchant, made his fortune as a privateer and slave-trader. The De Wolfes were, in fact, the largest slave-trading dynasty in early America. From 1769 to 1820, the family brought an estimated 10,000 people from the west coast of Africa to auction blocks in Charleston and other southern U.S. and Caribbean ports, as well as to their own sugar plantations in Cuba, and into their homes.

Of course, none of this excuses any of Charleston's abominable history in the trade, nor heals the scars that linger.

But all this had nothing to do with me. I felt no guilt for having been born a middle-class Southerner of humble ancestry, mostly descended from small farmers. And as distasteful as I found all this retrograde preoccupation with the past, I came to realize that other facets of Charleston history were engrossing, including that many vehemently opposed the slave trade and secession here and in the rest of the South.

That was the lesson of *Rebels in the Making: The Secession Crisis and the Birth of the Confederacy* (Oxford University Press, 2020), an eye-opening account by UNC history professor William L. Barney.

I also discovered that Charleston had an undercurrent of liberalism and acceptance (sometimes grudging) of those "from off," which distinguished it from many other southern communities. It was, among other things, a college town. And while The Citadel was a bastion of traditionalism (albeit with some "subversive" professors), the College of Charleston, Trident Technical College, and Baptist College (soon to be renamed Charleston Southern) generally bucked the prevailingly conservative atmosphere.

And yet, imagine my disbelief when I returned to the newsroom after an interview one day that first summer and was told by an editor that the images the photographer had taken could not be used. Why? Because they depicted a white man and a Black man touching (they had shaken hands). I was dumbfounded. This was 1980, not 1940. What the hell? I protested, and promptly was shot down.

Perhaps I should not have been surprised. There were also quite a few local clubs and restaurants where African-Americans were not allowed entry. I had experienced little of this in Virginia or Florida—snobbery, yes, but not this degree of overt racial discrimination. But in Charleston I even witnessed prejudice *within* the black community between dark-skinned and light-skinned individuals, though it was more subterranean. Reverse racism also reared its ugly head now and then. Tribalism is catching.

It does no good to say, as a friend once did, there is no equivalency (between racism and reverse racism). Perhaps not. But how many incidents does it take before it is wrong?

It was a relief when I saw the stones of this edifice start to crumble. Speeding it along had been the election of Joseph P. Riley, Jr. as mayor in 1975. Although he never met a developer he didn't like, Riley would go on to serve 10 terms, and under his leadership the city underwent a period of positive political and cultural transformation. A key element in the artistic rebirth of Charleston was the introduction of the Spoleto Festival USA (introduced in 1977), which quickly grew into one of the most renowned arts festivals in the world.

Riley and then-College of Charleston President Theodore Stern were major players in attracting celebrated operatic composer and festival founding director Gian Carlo Menotti to the city, creating the *Festival dei Due Mondi* (Festival of the Two Worlds) connecting Charleston and Spoleto, Italy. This was the first step in restoring the city's reputation as a center of the arts in the South, last seen during the Charleston Renaissance (1917-1941), a groundswell of creativity between the two world wars that not only resuscitated the arts in the city but was among the earliest seats of American's historic preservation movement.

Another pivotal event pushed by Riley was the opening in 1986 of the luxury lodging, shopping and dining locus that was the Omni Hotel and Charleston Place. Situated in the heart of the city, or rather becoming its heart, the Omni Hotel and its satellites greatly accelerated the process of Charleston becoming a global tourist destination. More, it furthered a culinary revolution that had begun a few years earlier, rapidly turning the city into the foodie mecca it is today.

By the time Riley retired in 2016, the town I'd been introduced to in 1980 was unrecognizable.

Meanwhile, newspaper management, though still beholding to the old gentry and its concerns to a degree, gradually entered the late 20th century, and I like to think I helped prod it in some small way, through my writing if nothing else. I made the transition from sports to features quite readily, and got a kick out of writing about anything and everything under the sun: human interest stories, profiles, consumer news, science, business, etc. I even tried my hand as a humorist and (guest) editorial writer. It was challenging venturing cold into five or six stories a week, often not knowing a thing about the subject, or having only superficial knowledge. My job got even more demanding when the responsibilities of book review editor were added a year after my arrival.

Doing the Charleston (Second Dance)

Feature writing certainly afforded me the most variety I've had in my working life. Over the course of 10 years I interviewed hundreds of scientists, lawyers, physicians, builders, teachers, business people, carpenters, politicians, miners, homemakers, craftsmen, social activists, chefs, collectors, environmentalists, theater owner/operators, farmers, impresarios, models, architects, taxi drivers, publishers, transportation professionals, pilots, recyclers, editors, booksellers, electricians, caterers, police officers, travel agents, radio and TV personalities, reporters, historians and, well, you name it.

I recall one week that encapsulated the whole decade, in which I interviewed a plasma physicist from Cal Tech, a rural wood carver, a would-be Hollywood starlet, a snake handler, a guy with a one-fifth scale railroad in his back yard, and former New York City Mayor John Lindsey. Every week was a fresh and unpredictable reboot.

Naming a group of favorite interviews from this feature-writing period would be difficult. But one profile was especially memorable, an interview with the gifted cultural anthropologist Ethel-Jane Bunting. A *grande dame* when I met her, well into her 80s, she was distinguished in aspect but warmed by a glint of mischief in her eye, and still possessed of a remarkable curiosity. Her home was a veritable museum of artifacts from around the world, from the Caspian Sea to the lands of the Maya—many of which she had unearthed. And she had stories to tell. My, what stories.

At age 14 she had embodied that all-too-familiar role of a young woman of her era whose ambitions were dismissed because she aspired to work in "a man's field." The fellow who gave her the basilisk gaze was none other than famed British archaeologist Howard Carter, discoverer of the tomb of Tutankhamun in 1922.

Bunting, fascinated and thrilled by Carter's finding, had been on a Mediterranean cruise with her mother when she chanced to be seated beside him at a formal tea in Cairo.

"I turned to him and, with all the courage I could muster, asked 'Sir, how does a girl become an archaeologist?' He looked at me with the most scornful expression on his face and said, 'Marry one.' I felt like crying."

A lifetime later, on this bright spring day in 1990, she was laughing. The last laugh. She had never become an archaeologist, but she had never stopped digging.

Born in New Orleans, Ethel-Jane Westfeldt was educated at Tulane University and Oxford. She was the daughter of George G. Westfeldt, a successful coffee importer, and Martha Gasquet Westfeldt, a formidable woman who had been decorated with the French Legion of Honor for her help in repatriating French sailors interned in New Orleans during World War II. She died the day Gen. Charles De Gaulle was to arrive in the Big Easy to honor her.

Young Ethel-Jane grew up in privileged surroundings, with advantages she never took for granted. Her parents expected much of her, but she already yearned to achieve. At Tulane she met Mayan scholar Frank Blum, head of what was then known as the Department of Middle American Research.

"But I knew I was too young—and too female—to be permitted to go on a dig with him. So I asked to come up and clean his museum room, read the materials, and meet some of the archaeologists. That's really how it all started for me."

She went to Oxford to study Egyptology, but the professor had withdrawn from the course by the time she arrived on campus and Bunting had to change her field of study, which proved pivotal. "I had a delightful time at Oxford; I didn't learn a thing," she told me. "But I gained enough to give me a background for what I would later do." She also gained a husband.

A year after graduating, she married economist Frederick H. Bunting of Pennsylvania (d. 1982), whom she had met at Oxford, traveling widely with him while he was employed by the U.S. State Department's Agency for International Development. During several years in Pakistan, she made a study of the culture and historical artifacts of the Lower Sind Valley and Baluchistan and was commissioned by the Smithsonian Institution to collect materials for their exhibit on Sindhi culture. Her book *Sindhi Tombs and Textiles: The Persistence of Pattern,* was published in 1980, just one achievement in a long and accomplished career, which included a key civilian post with the O.S.S. (forerunner of the CIA) during World War II.

A great lady. A great life. And a splendid interview.

But let's backtrack a bit.

When I came to town in 1980, the Features editor at the *News and Courier* was Betsy Moye, daughter of the paper's longtime columnist, Frank Gilbreth, better known to Charlestonians as the resident man-about-town "Ashley Cooper" and author of the best-selling memoir *Cheaper by the Dozen.* For those not in the know, the Ashley and Cooper Rivers, which bound the Charleston peninsula, meet to form the Atlantic Ocean—though sticklers for history will counter that the rivers actually were named after Anthony Ashley Cooper, one of the eight Lords Proprietor of the Province of Carolina.

But Betsy was no case study in nepotism. She had the chops.

I owe her a lot. Because of Betsy, I spent the lion's share of my newspaper career covering two of my primary passions, books and movies. I was given the functional responsibility of book review editor in 1981, and though Mr. Gilbreth kept the title for a few more years, I did the work, which included recruiting and managing reviewers, assigning reviews and, of course, dealing with the publishing industry—all in *addition* to my feature writing. Apparently, I had made the strategic mistake of showing how much I *could* do.

For years, the newspaper had eschewed reviewing movies, largely for fear that negative critiques would irk movie theater owners who advertised with the *News and Courier*. But one day in 1982 Betsy informed me that I was being assigned to review the feature film based on a local monster legend, "Swamp Thing." It was a dreary little low-budget clunker, clumsily made, but also the beginning of what would become a fairly substantial film industry in the Lowcountry region and in the state.

For the next few years the paper reviewed movies sporadically. I shared the post with my coworkers Frank Jarrell and Fred Smith. We alternated, not one of us confident that this would become a regular thing. Frank soon became the chief arts writer, and Fred a TV columnist, which opened the door for me to assume the film critic-columnist role full time.

By 1991, the *News and Courier* had merged with its longtime companion the *Evening Post* to form the *Post and Courier*, and I was to hold the film position in conjunction with book coverage for the next 19 years. I like to believe I discharged that role with some distinction. (More on that, and the literary world, later).

Frank, the first person to befriend me in 1980, helped me move into my duplex apartment on James Island and, with his wife Chris and their two young daughters, Besse and Katie, adopted me into the fold. Frank and I were pretty close, especially after his divorce, and I hated to see him go when he left for California, then Mexico, then Bolivia, then Ecuador, where he died a happy man after fighting through many physical and emotional travails.

Not long after I met Frank, I enjoyed a large dose of serendipity. With the advent of the home VCR and videotapes, I was eager to put together a personal film library. Fortunately, the desire coincided with the debut of video stores in the city and the good fortune to meet Bob and Lynne Millenbine, proprietors of National Home Video, not only because I was able to assemble that library in short order, but because we have shared a close friendship of 40 years standing. It continues, despite Bob's untimely passing a few years ago.

As Luck Would Have It

Lynne, her daughter Stephanie, and son-in-law Eric Vanderhorst are all dear to me. I have spent more time in the company of the Millenbines than any other family, save my own. Others in their orbit became valued friends, above all Steve James, a great pal for many years now. I even forgive him for being a lawyer.

There are many other couples I've known for decades here that are special to me. The first are Skip and Sue Johnson. Skip was the city editor at the newspaper when we met, and Sue the chief fiction librarian at the main branch of the Charleston County Public Library. They had an unfailing knack for finding the coolest places to live in the city, and I've enjoyed all of them, especially when they were caretakers of South Carolina Society Hall, living in the coziest little apartment you ever saw, nestled in the back of an enormous building.

Skip and I have had thousands of entertaining conversations and arguments over the years, in newsrooms and in homes, and I always look forward to our get-togethers.

I met Frank and Phyllis Licciardi when I came to their home one day to conduct what would become one of my favorite interviews. Frank, a crooner during Depression-era Chicago and a tavern owner in Dubuque, Iowa, did not take up art seriously until his 50s. He became one of the finest painters in America, or anywhere else. No exaggeration. He was an earthy and amusingly profane sort of fellow, with a delightfully outsized personality and a peerless talent for living. He overcame numerous physical issues, including strokes and cancer, thumbing his nose at them for years before he and death finally struck a bargain. His work continues to dominate my extensive art collection.

Phyllis was, and is, equally outgoing, but more the calm within the storm who had raised heaven knows how many kids. She is a gem, a straightforward Midwesterner, and my appreciation of her wit and wisdom grows with every passing year.

You seldom have a choice as to who your neighbors might be, but sometimes you just get lucky. One day in 1983, Kevin Keeler and Annie

Utegg bought the duplex next door, having originally lived in a large group house on the peninsula after moving here from Upstate New York.

Kevin had been a cook on a large "boomer" submarine during his Navy years and, until he and Annie had their two sons, Emmett and Wade, probably could not prepare a meal for fewer than 400 people. When we met, Kevin was a civilian employee at the Charleston Navy Base, serving as a hazardous materials foreman. One, I might add, who could paper his walls with commendations had he wished. His capacity for innovation was a trait that characterized his entire career, including his years almost single-handedly revamping and running Cedar Island National Wildlife Refuge in eastern North Carolina.

In the mid-1990s, the Keelers moved into a venerable, 100-year-old rural home in Gloucester, N.C., near the southern approach to the Outer Banks. But before that they were legends in Charleston. Annie was, and is, the empress of all Earth mothers (a.k.a., the "Sweet Goddess of Love and Beer"), a gifted artist who shares her husband's extraordinary knack for making friends with almost everybody. They were always the bright star around which many a human planet orbited.

Although they were many years my junior, they always struck me as throwbacks to the Sixties, gentle-spirited "hippies" whose main purpose in life was to enjoy it, and be useful.

For many years in Charleston the Keelers held an annual Blind Pig Pickin' (complete with a kids' "pignata") for what seemed like 200 of their close personal friends, a feast that was resumed in Gloucester. Altogether it enjoyed a memorable 30-year run and was always a highlight of the year. But the coolest thing about living next door to them, apart from their company and that of Annie's sister Chris, was the fact that talented musicians could drop by at any time for impromptu sessions. A number of them were touring pros. But amateur or pro, all were good. It was always a pleasure hanging out at Casa Keeler, in both the Carolinas.

Ben Moise began reviewing books for the *Post and Courier* while he was still a staunch conservation officer with the South Carolina Department of Natural Resources—his book *Ramblings of a Lowcountry Game Warden* (USC Press, 2008) is a must-read—and both he and his uber-gracious wife Anne—a classiest of Southern ladies—continued reviewing after he retired in 2002. Ben is also a talented cook and travel writer. We were always cordial, but as time went on we got closer, and for some years now I have counted them among my most valued friends. The annual gathering in their home in conjunction with the Southeastern Wildlife Exposition, an unrivaled and truly astounding feast, remains my favorite Charleston event ever. It is no more, but the memories and tastes linger.

Other couples that have secured a place either in my heart or my admiration (or both) include Annie Rousseau and the late Richard Stern, Rick and Krista Dausener, George and Christine Finnan, Wesley and the late Judy Moore, Wesley Moore and new wife Caroline Traugott, Dawn Brazell and Alan Seim, Cara and Marty Bluford, Cathy and Alan Holmes, Peter and Marjory Wentworth, Tony Brown and Nancy Groh, Bert and Lucille Keller, Geverts and Rita Hollings, Rodney Rogers and Sharon Graci, Buddy and Cathy Jenrette, Jack Bass and Nathalie DuPree, Dana and Virginia Beach, Mike and Anne Adair, Kyra and Rob Morris, David Wyatt and Alyssa Neely, Katie and Tim Mahoney, David and Marti Adams, and Suzi and Wayne Hardwick.

You can't live in one town for more than 40 years or work at one paper for 32 of them and not have a wide circle of friends and acquaintances, many of them former colleagues at the *Post and Courier* like the inimitable Fred Smith, Angie Blackburn, Walter Allread, Mike Mooneyham, David Quick, Dan Conover and Janet Edens, Stephanie Harvin, Tony Brown, Vickie Hood, Wade Spees, Elsa McDowell, Brian Hicks, Laura Bradshaw, Adam Parker, Wevonita Minis, Steve Mullins, Judy Watts, Eddie Fennell, Charles Rowe, Prentiss Findley, Laura Peck, Herb Frazier, Gene Sapakoff, Christine Randall, Frank Wooten, Teresa Taylor, Tommy Braswell, Tyrone Walker, Leroy Burnell, Roger Gaskill, Shirley Greene, David MacDougal, Mindy Spar, Gil Guerry, Lisa Dennis, Fred and Brenda Rindge, Schuyler Kropf, Susan Sanders, Andy Lions, Robie Scott, Mike Green, Marsha Guerard, Jim

Bill Thompson

Parker, Pam Liles, Brad Nettles, Pat Jones, Bo Peterson, Libby Wallace, the late Ken Burger, Cleve O'Quinn, Susan Sanders, Tony Bartleme, Lisa Justis, Bryce Donovan, Kristen Hankla, Schuyler Kropf, Peggy McIntyre, Dave Munday, Tom Spain, Barbara Williams, Phil Bowman, Rick Nelson, Darlene Gardner, John McDermott, Harriett McLeod, Chuck Boyd, Betsy Miller, Robert Behre, Bill Hawkins, Larry Tarleton, Grover McNeil, and the late, great Jack McCray. (I know I'm forgetting some people. Sorry, folks).

Two gents deserve special mention. Though our politics were dissimilar, Mike Bonafield and I became quite close. Mike was an editorial writer for the paper, and a most unusual fellow, with an unconventional combination of expertise in the American Civil War and Czarist Russia. He was a handsome, suave, gracious, worldly chap with charm to burn (especially with the ladies). Mike had been a foreign correspondent for a number of years in France and the Soviet Union (where he had a few brushes with the KGB). He was a man of contrasts, staunchly conservative politically and proudly of the Greek Orthodox persuasion (he thought Roman Catholicism too namby-pamby), but a tolerant, free-and-easy sort personally. What stood out to me was how he listened, really *listened*, to opposing points of view, weighing and considering and giving an argument a fair hearing. It was not grudging. It was respectful, and something he believed in.

Today, in our polarized society? Don't get me started. Few possess Mike's openness to ideas that didn't conform to his own.

Gent Two was the *other* Bill Thompson at the paper, a staff artist and exceptional political cartoonist who could have been among the best in the country had management had the intelligence to give him free rein, or at least some creative latitude. They thought him too liberal. He wasn't. He was just incisive, and funny, while management was (in my view) staid and timid. The soldier who served two tours of duty in Vietnam and the protestor (me) who refused to fight in a ludicrous war, strangely (or perhaps not too strangely) had common ground years after it ended. Bill felt betrayed by the war. I felt vindicated. At the same time, both of us were deeply saddened that so many lives had been lost for so misguided a conflict. Bill also had a touch of survivor's guilt, believing he was living on borrowed time. As a consequence, he seldom gave thought to his health, which proved to be his undoing.

Bill was a fine illustrator and painter in his off hours, living in a proverbial "garret" with a tiny loft in North Charleston. Many a day I spent there chewing the fat and discovering how many unexpected similarities and parallel paths our lives had had -- apart from the military. Brothers from different mothers. His charm was offhand and insinuating compared to Mike's, but most women found his shaggy dog looks and the romance of the "starving" artist irresistible. Maternal instinct, I guess. Amusingly, readers often confused the two of us. Sometimes we'd get praise (or scorn) for each other's work.

Mike and Bill are gone now. The world is poorer.

"Civilians" for whom I have fond feelings and memories include the late, great Craig Wright (*I Can Hear Angels Calling*), Susan Ackerman, Price Robinson, the late Jeff Johnson, Rick Hatcher, Billy Baldwin, Margaret Ford, Candice Suggars, the late Dottie Frank, Gary Smith, Maria Cordoba, the late Phillip Sheehan, Morgan Brynnan, Jeff Poole, Eugene Platt, Susan Sully, the late Dick Côté, Leigh Murray, David Boatwright, Josephine Humphreys, Jonathan Haupt, Alex Moore, Paula Watkins, Bret Lott, Tina Helm, the late Pat Conroy, Kathy Clark, Glenn Burns, Barbara Barnes, Robert Morris, the late Tripp Compton, Mary Alice Monroe, Tom Blagden, Nicole Seitz, the late Bill Shoemaker, Alice Gray Gregory, the late Lee Norvell, Marcie Marzluff, the late Dick Reed, the late Frances Monaco, Harlan Greene, Dori Sanders, Jim Hutchisson, Douglas Gleaton, and my fellow members of the Thomas Street Book Club, not least Buddy Jenrette, Paul O'Brien and David Adams.

Candice Suggars, as sweet as her name, has been a particularly delightful friend and companion over the past two decades. We lost touch for a few years before bumping into each other at a film festival 15 years ago, but renewed our acquaintance and have been great pals ever since. As a tutor of children, I'd venture that she has no equal.

Above all there's Lynne Riding, an unusually gifted artist who left a successful career in London to follow her then-husband to the States. I'm glad she came, and stayed. Lynne grew up in Wales and gets homesick from time to time, understandably. Today she remains one of my best and closest friends. More on her later.

Rarae aves all.

Then there are those from "off." Bob Nunnenkamp, my old college buddy) and I reconnected in the early 2000s, not that we had lost touch altogether. I met his wife Judy when they drove down from Charlotte to visit me in December of 2006, just in time for an exceedingly rare Charleston snow "storm." It lent a magical quality to the reunion, and since then we have spent a lot of time together, often on mountain hikes.

CHARLESTON AND SOUTH CAROLINA. My life here has been a continuing adjustment (but, then, isn't that the nature of life?). Given my temperament, I have often found things to criticize in the city and state that has been my home longer than anyplace else, but also much to praise. And apart from the many kind people I've met over the years, one thing I must applaud is our parks and recreational spaces. We need *something* to deflect us from the unremitting flatness of the landscape, and we've got it in abundance.

As someone who has visited and stayed in state and national parks around the country, South Carolina's are among the best. Just in the Lowcountry area, my favorite places to loll about and commune with nature are two urban oases—Charles Towne Landing State Historic Park and Hampton Park—and a wealth of other city and county parks: Caw Caw Plantation, North Charleston Riverfront Park, Santee Coastal Reserve, Cypress Gardens, Old Santee Canal Park, the Audubon Swamp Garden, Middleton Place, Magnolia Gardens, James Island County Park at Folly Beach, Palmetto Islands County Park, the beach at Sullivan's Island, Biedler Forest, and Pitt Street Bridge Park. Just thought I'd say something nice.

I am less enthralled with the prevailing attitudes towards land *use* in the region.

As Luck Would Have It

In his regard, I have to give a shout out to the work of Dana and Virginia Beach, founders of the Coastal Conservation League, and, by extension, to those whom they have turned over day-to-day operations after decades fighting the good fight. The CCL remains a bulwark against urban sprawl, environmental degradation, ill-advised highway projects (which, after a temporary easing of traffic congestion, only worsen the situation), and other depredations, problems almost entirely driven by real estate developers, city and county councils dominated by current or former development professionals, or members sympathetic to their philosophy. As I write this in the fall of 2023, there is no political will to stop or even slow the rampant, out-of-control over-building, not only on Peninsular Charleston, which is increasingly a parking lot, but throughout the Greater Charleston area. Quite the contrary. The heedless mantra of "growth, growth, growth"—a sorry masterpiece of short-term thinking—never takes into account the consequences. Or as Edward Abbey so succinctly put it, "Growth for its own sake is the philosophy of the cancer cell."

And this at a time when we desperately need affordable housing for people—another critical problem to which the various councils generally give lip service. Instead, we get luxury hotels. That's why three years ago I volunteered with CAJM, the Charleston Area Justice Ministry, whose members advocate (tirelessly) not only for housing but for environmental justice, equity in affordable health care, educational opportunity, and an end to racial profiling, among other issues. It is a thorn in the side of forces who only want to preserve the status quo. It's an uphill climb, frequently frustrating, yet CAJM tries hard to work within the system.

But back to our story. Namely, *Me*.

In the mid-eighties I broke my sacred vow not to date anyone with whom I worked. When a news-side copy editor named Harriett Dockery was assigned to edit the book page—or rather, re-edit after me—a friendship developed despite our differing attitudes on the inviolable nature of grammar and syntax, or lack of same. I was definitely in the latter camp, having cavalierly played with words and language as a sportswriter. She was a purist, and persnickety —a "school marm" at heart. At the same time, her knowledge of contemporary fiction, which did not appeal as much to me, was far more comprehensive, and she had the eye of a hawk.

A romance began, despite my apprehensions about possible office conflict down the road, and about getting involved with *another* young mother. Harriett never let on if she shared those apprehensions. But it was an amiable, mutually sustaining relationship for some time. We kept our coupledom confidential for the most part, not wanting to be fodder for office gossip. We spent a great deal of time just gabbing and having fun, and she would indulge some of my less outgoing interests, like playing chess. She claims never to have never let me win at the game, though my spotless record against her leaves me dubious.

Our relationship survived until she realized I was not inclined to get too serious or, more to the point, when she was offered a plum job in Dallas. Get along little doggie (in affectionate cowboy terms), and happy trails. Harriett and I remain friends today, seeing each other from time to time here or at her home in Charlotte, N.C.

Which brings up the subject of what has been a real blessing in my life: Romances that eventually morphed into enduring friendships. I have never married or had children, though I came close with my college sweetheart, Anne. Who was it that said, "Marriage is an institution, and I don't want to be institutionalized"? My friends have always been my family. It's true that from time to time I experience a mild sense of guilt that I am the last of the line on my father's side, the last entry in this set of Thompsons. It doesn't feel much like a distinction. No such issue on Mom's side of the family, with generations of offspring aplenty.

Mom and Dad never pressed me to have children. Well, Dad a little. I always felt there was time, if I really wanted them. I just never did. I remember two things Mom said. The first was that the only reason to have children was because you desperately wanted them. The second was that she feared I might regret never having had this fundamental human experience. She might have been right on the latter, but it's academic now.

As Luck Would Have It

With rare exceptions, and to this day, all of the women with whom I have been romantically involved in my adult life—not that there have been legions—have remained good friends. A *new* ladyfriend might question if there was unfinished business with past paramours, but eventually learns this isn't the case. How lucky can you get, right? But I give unwavering loyalty in return. Why jettison a perfectly good friendship just because a romance has run its course?

In the summer of 1986, I met Griffen Jack. At the time she was donating her "vacation" time to teaching at the International Business School of the University of South Carolina in Columbia. Teaching, I might add, people with graduate degrees, of which she had none. What she had was an extremely sharp mind, expertise in world affairs—and an enviable flair for art. Originally, Griff had trained for the diplomatic corps but instead had devoted her career being a Peace Corps trainer in the African country of Cameroon and later a first responder/team leader for relief organizations like Mercy Corps. I believe she is still at it today, though we have been out of touch in recent years.

Griff came from a prominent family, one might even say "aristocratic" after a fashion, and I wondered, at first, if her involvement was a matter of *noblesse oblige*. It was not, at least not strictly. It was the simple need to be of help to those in distress, typically in the aftermath of calamities.

We had an affair that summer, a very practical sort of affair, really. She was there, I was there. and it just sort of happened organically. No one was in love. Still, when the summer ended and she was back to work, I missed her. I had become friendly with her parents, who divided their time between residences in Asheville and the Lowcountry, and we all stayed in touch for a long while. Occasionally—usually at Christmas—Griff would come for a visit and we would catch up with each other during her parents' annual yuletide party at Upper Oaks, their home in the North Charleston enclave of Yeaman's Hall.

Enter, stage right, one of the most interesting and sophisticated women I've ever met, Beatrice Stiglitz, a professor of languages at the College of Charleston who defined the term multi-lingual. Born in Russia and raised in Romania, her family moved to New York when she was 16. I met her while covering one of the small festivals of French films she organized at the school and gradually we began to see more of each other.

It blossomed into a full-scale romance that lasted not quite two years before morphing into a fond and lasting friendship. She was an amazing person, so generous, intelligent, and amusing, especially her quirky (sometimes perplexing) way of looking at things and her abiding passion for cats—drawings and paintings and figurines of which festooned her townhouse. Oddly, she never seemed to own a live cat, content to feed and amuse the wild ones.

Sunday afternoons in her home we called "International Days," during which one or both of us would field calls from friends in various countries of Europe. If I answered the phone, it always made me feel a little provincial that whoever was calling would immediately switch to perfect English when it became clear I was not fluent in French or Spanish, German or Dutch, Romanian or Greek.

Parenthetically, my chief regrets today are that I've yet to learn another language or master a musical instrument. Being a singer in the past doesn't really count. It's not too late, I suppose. I'm not sure I have the facility, but at the not-so-tender age of 75 I'd better have at it soon.

Beatrice fought a valiant, long-term battle with breast cancer, having beaten it back twice before finally succumbing. This is what I said at her service:

> *"If we are very fortunate in our lifetimes we are privileged to meet and befriend a few genuinely remarkable people, individuals whose vitality, curiosity, zest for living, and contributions to their communities are models of a life well lived.*
>
> *It is difficult to imagine the world without Beatrice Stiglitz's high spirits, high principles, impeccable taste, and good humor, though the echo of these will last for many years. The influence she had on us was incalculable. The pleasure she gave us was in*

equal measure to the provocative intelligence which challenged our assumptions.

I know this: She knew the meaning of friendship. She valued it greatly. She will always be a part of me, someone who inspires the better angels of our sometimes cantankerous natures, but encourages the leavening of impish mischief. I am reminded of a quote from the wife of the late New York Times book critic Anatole Broyard, who said of her husband, "He was alive when he died." As was Beatrice. What better epitaph could one have?

The Hindus have a phrase for it: a large soul. Beatrice was all of that. Larger than life, too. I've never known a person of more courage or less pretense, of more wit or less rancor. She never wasted a day. Not one. Like Emerson, she wished each hour to be as days, loaded, fragrant. There were, for all of us in her company."

I could say much the same about other people I've been fortunate to have in my life.

Well before Beatrice had passed, but after we had transitioned from romance to friendship, I embarked on a new romance with another artist, Barbara Whitley. Her day job was as a lab technician at Roper Hospital. Her passion, however, was painting. I still have some of her work in my home. I think her mother was rather partial to me and might have wished that Barb and I were angling toward something more permanent. But neither Barb nor I wanted that at the time—she also wanted kids -- and things finally came to an amicable end after six months or so, if memory serves.

The personal turning point, the biggest in my adult life, arrived not long after, at the very time I was trying to quit smoking. As it happens, I was writing a story on smoking cessation methods offered by the American Lung Association, the American Cancer Society and other, local organizations. Among them was a program being considered for adoption by the Medical University of South Carolina in its treatment protocols, and it was this one for which I chose to be a guinea pig. It was run by the unlikely combination of a male nurse and a retired used car salesman. Their promise: Go through the program for one week, one hour a day at their facility, and if at the end of that time you still wanted a cigarette, your $300 fee would be refunded, no questions asked.

Of course, being a journalist doing a story, the fee was waived for me, so I didn't even have the motivation of money on the line. I had been a heavy smoker for years, upwards of two and a half packs a day at the pinnacle of my addiction, and had tried on several occasions to kick the habit—only to find the methods advocated a kind of slow torture. This new approach was different, a gentle form of aversion therapy. The day before starting the program I resolved to smoke so many cigarettes that, by way of setting the stage, I was sick to my stomach from them and ready.

Those taking "the cure" would be zipped up inside the equivalent of an enormous, translucent garment bag. One sat in a simple chair facing a TV monitor, wearing the lead apron they use at dental offices when taking X-rays. On your lap was a large cookie sheet on which sat a very big glass ashtray filled to the brim with foul-smelling cigarette butts. Alongside was a pack of fresh cigarettes. The patient was told to open the pack, light a cigarette and puff on it until the enclosure filled with smoke—but *no*t to inhale. Meanwhile, the monitor showed both cartoon images and repulsive photos of actual smokers whose bodies had been ravaged by the habit. As you were watching these, beneath the threshold of (conscious) awareness were "subliminal cuts" that flicked quickly on and off the screen saying things like "Disease," "Cancer," "Death." In turn, these inputs were reinforced by the male nurse sitting outside your station, talking in a slow, sonorous voice about the dangers of smoking and the freedom conferred by quitting. This was further augmented, mid-week, by a documentary film featuring actual cowboys who had been hired as virile "Marlboro men" for a series of popular TV and print ads. All of those interviewed now had lung cancer, and lawyers for the tobacco industry tried diligently to have the documentary banned. They failed.

The final day in the "bag," the nurse took my blood pressure when I sat down and showed me the results. Then for the first time that week, I was asked to smoke a cigarette and inhale. He repeated the blood pressure reading and it had skyrocketed—as clear and irrefutable a marker as one could have. At the end of the week, I sat across a desk from the retired used car salesman. He slid three $100 bills across one side of the table and a pack of cigarettes across the other. If I wanted a cigarette, he said, the $300 was mine—not a refund (since I hadn't paid a dime), but a gift. I declined. I haven't wanted a cigarette since.

The program was more than 85-percent successful, but in the end MUSC did not adopt it. To this day, I am not entirely sure if it was the program that was the main factor that helped me quit, the fact that I was finally psychologically ready, or a combination of both.

Anyway, shortly after completing the program in the spring of 1988, into the newspaper offices came an ex-English major and would-be book critic, hopeful of getting a chance—the aforementioned turning point. She had only recently quit drinking *an*d smoking when she ambled up to my desk. But if you think we were an immediate study in shared empathy, you'd be mistaken.

Rosemary Michaud introduced herself and asked if I needed any new reviewers (we *always* needed new reviewers). I was in a bad mood that day, and she was put off by my impatience (as well as the melodramatic snapping of a pencil. Even so, I signed her up on the spot. Thirty-five years later she is still reviewing books for the *Post and Courier*, often brilliantly.

A physical therapy assistant, also at Roper Hospital, she was a petite, infinitely cuter and more approachable version of Susan Sontag, her dark brown hair judiciously flecked with gray—this was before Rosemary became a blonde—framing mischievous eyes that almost lured the eye away from her trim figure. I was attracted immediately. Matters were complicated in her life at the time, but eventually we fell into a love affair that lasted for nine years, six of them living together in the ideally located South Windermere neighborhood, a block from our favorite haunt, the Mediterranean Deli.

I even fell in love with Ro's cat, Bojayka, who generously accepted me (I got special dispensation because I am a Leo).

In some respects, Mme. Michaud and I were/are polar opposites. The morning person and the night owl. The Irish-Catholic political junkie and the agnostic political cynic. The woman who missed New England and the guy for whom home was wherever he happened to be. Ms. Let-It-Ride vs. Mr. Fix-It. But we also had much in common. Movies, books, senses of humor that dovetailed nicely, an appreciation for most things British, and a love of history, to name some of our confluences.

The lady from Haverhill, Mass., and the dude from Lexington, N.C., made North and South find common ground (my sensibilities were more "Northern" anyway), even if we didn't always see eye to eye. Those nine years were among the happiest of my life. Especially memorable was our trip across Italy in 1996, and it was in a fragrant lemon and olive grove near our hotel in the city of Sorrento that the most romantic interlude of my adult life played out. It was glorious.

Despite this journey and many other wonderful times together, our differences finally overtook our affections. Deeply saddened, we finally broke up in 1998, 25 years ago I'm startled to say, yet still travel together on occasion, and rarely fail to see each other at least once a week. Something that hasn't always sat well with later girlfriends who didn't know the score. The score being: I do not abandon friends, for any reason.

Rosemary was then, and remains today, my best and closest friend. I have dated and had relationships with several other women since our break-up, including a few whirlwind romances and one long-term one with a lovely lass named Leslee Power, who also remains a very good friend. But Rosemary is the only woman I have ever truly loved, and it's hard to imagine life without her in it. Some stubborn mutual friends still hold out hope that we will get back together. We dissuade them from that notion, knowing that in too many ways we are like oil and water, that the past is past, and that trying to rekindle a romance long over would probably doom the friendship we treasure. That said, we've never lost our regard or our feelings for each other. And never will.

Doing the Charleston (Third Dance)

Of all the people who were most influential in my career path, not to mention my appreciation for professionalism, ethics, and personal courage, Bob Cox is right at the top. For years this affable, charming Englishman was the editor-in-chief of the *Buenos Aires Herald*, South America's premier English-language daily.

Surprisingly, the newspaper was owned by the *Post and Courier's* parent company, then called the Evening Post, Inc. (now Evening Post Industries). Bob was and is a man of unassailable principles, a model journalist. Throughout his tenure, he stood for probity and responsibility, and expected it of others. In Argentina, he was in a difficult position in which to uphold these ideals. The country was rife with corruption and violence in the 1970s. Because Cox consistently dared to oppose the policies and actions of the ruling military junta (1976-1983), he was detained and briefly jailed. But the threats continued upon his release, usually against his family. Partly at the insistence of Evening Post, Inc. owner Peter Manigault, Cox and his family left Buenos Aires for Charleston in 1979.

In 2005, the Buenos Aires legislature cited Cox for his work and strength of character. Three years later his son David published the book titled *Dirty Secrets, Dirty War: The Exile of Robert J. Cox*, detailing the near state of siege his father and family endured. Those years also were brought to the screen in 2016 with *Messenger On A White Horse,* an exemplary documentary by Jayson McNamara recounting Cox's role in exposing the dictatorship's assassinations of the "disappeared," a horror also portrayed in Luis Puenzo's haunting Argentine feature film *The Official Story* (1985).

Bob and I met in 1981. His office in the *News and Courier* newsroom was directly behind my desk, and gradually we got to know each other. He supported me in numerous ways, at one point offering sage counsel in turning down a job with the *Washington Times* in Washington, D.C. Though it was a much bigger paper and in a genuinely cosmopolitan city—as opposed to Charleston's veneer of same of the time—it would have been a step back, especially given the Times' rather questionable reputation at the time.

I am proud to be a family friend, and see Bob, his wife Maud, and their children as often as I can. Evenings in their home often have an international flavor, with guests from many cultures.

By 1981, I had added books to my features reporting responsibilities, though Gibreath remained the titular book review editor. Covering books (and later, film) for the Charleston paper meant having a local, regional, national, and international perspective. While some felt I should have concentrated solely on local and state or "Southern" writers, I refused to be parochial about it. The Charleston area had residents from all over the country and, while they were doubtless interested in the literature of their adopted home, I was convinced that was not the only literature to which they were drawn. Of course, I would interview accomplished local authors when they had a book coming out, and secure reviewers for those books whenever possible, just as I would cover local film figures, support personnel, and industry news in the state (the latter when I could actually get someone to go on the record).

But I have to confess that, with my experience covering the "big leagues" as a sportswriter, privately I was drawn to the best of the best, which required a more outward gaze. Just as I had the privilege of doing interviews with some of the world's finest actors, directors, screenwriters and cinematographers, I also had the pleasure of interviewing many of the most consummate novelists and non-fiction writers of the day.

Don't misunderstand, South Carolina in general and the Charleston area in particular had some very fine writers indeed, equal to any, but so many authors of note came through town on national book tours, and so many New York publicists approached me for interviews and reviews, that it was hard to resist extending my view.

But whatever the approach, it was a public trust and I always regarded it as such. I always tried to keep foremost in mind the importance of books, and why they endure, even if they are destined, eventually, for digital form alone. As the late, great historian Barbara Tuchman wrote so succinctly, "Without books, history is silent, literature dumb, science crippled, thought and speculation at a standstill. Without books, the development of civilization would have been impossible. They are engines of change, windows in the world, and lighthouses erected in the sea of time. They are companions, teachers, magicians, bankers of the treasure of the mind. Books are humanity in print."

Could anyone say it better? I would only add that they are our one true time machine, through which writers long dead can still speak to us, directly.

Even though book review editors were besieged on all sides by publishing house publicists and personal reps looking for coverage for their authors, dealing with the publishing industry was vastly less stressful than with the film world. Publishers were of the opinion that a dollar spent in Poughkeepsie was the same as one spent in Manhattan, or L.A., or Montevideo, and more often than not they were only too happy to fulfill your requests for an author interview. I estimate I did more than 600 of them over 32 years.

In terms of reviews, I had a number of reliable (unpaid) reviewers, but always sought more. Rosemary was one of these stalwarts, usually of nonfiction, with a first-rate grasp of politics and history. But for 20-plus years my secret weapon was the aforementioned Cathy Holmes, an English prof at the College of Charleston who was, as is, one of the most widely read people I know. She always reviewed the most demanding and significant works of fiction.

She would come into the office at least once a week, chatting for a while, asking about movies I'd just seen (and occasionally getting a sneak peek at a review). She would leave with an armload of books, and I'd have a review of the first tome in short order. And not just any review. Cathy's prose is incisive, knowing, and melodious, having nothing in common with typical academic writing apart from thoroughness. One editor told me he would have sooner fired me than lose her contributions. She's still at it, and the *Post and Courier's* readers are the beneficiaries.

By contrast, trying to get information from movie studios or the South Carolina Film Office was like breaking into Fort Knox with a ball-peen hammer. While the reps at the affiliated PR outfits, as in Atlanta, were consistently affable and reliable in providing press kits and scheduling private screenings, the industry in general cared mainly about what your paper's circulation was, how large a market you were in, and so on.

In other words, if you weren't the *New York Times*, or a glossy national magazine, they wouldn't give you the time of day. Interviews with the stars? Dream on, unless your paper sent you to Atlanta or New York for press junkets, which I got to attend only a handful of times. You were lucky if the gatekeepers of motion pictures would confirm that the sun rose in the east and set in the west. Fortunately, I was able to enlist the aid of a couple of Deep Throats within the industry, who shall remain nameless.

This wall of secrecy was especially true of movies filming in the Charleston area. Confidentiality was the posture. As was paranoia. So afraid that a local journalist would hear something they were not intended to know, or witness a spat between stars and directors that would wind up in some scandal sheet, the so-called unit publicist on set (a.k.a., anti-publicist) would clamp down on all information, promise the moon in terms of interviews, but delay and delay, delivering little or nothing. Meanwhile, my editors would get more and more impatient with me, wondering why I could not get on the set and interview the stars. Well, I managed to be a presence on sets often enough, not that it was terribly rewarding.

After you'd had been on a few, movie sets were boring. In contrast to telefilm or TV series sets, which are a scene of brisk, bustling motion, feature film shoots were a lot of hurry up and wait: hours on end of inactivity. While I waited for a moment of an actor or director's time, often in vain, your work kept piling up back at the office. Maybe I would get a few minutes with one of the actors or tech crew, maybe I wouldn't, though some film companies were more open than others. Some even welcomed you. It was always a surprise when they did, but appreciated.

One publicist was the antithesis of this resistance: South Carolina-born publicist Cara White, whose career spans her years in New York with the agency Clein & White, and her ongoing work representing the Public Broadcasting System (PBS). A film industry veteran, she has also handled publicity for many feature films. It was because of her irresistible charm, insider's persuasiveness, and persistence that I was granted several memorable star interviews. Today, one of my favorite parties of the year remains Cara's and husband Marty Bluford's Oscar fete.

Sometimes I'd benefit from coalescence with a famous actor whose shields I might never have penetrated were it not for the fact he or she had written a memoir and the publisher was keen to have its author interviewed.

I managed to secure or stumble into a lot of interviews on my own. Witness my exercise in unapologetic name-dropping at the end of this book.

Watching and reviewing films, however, was the real joy. All in all, I reviewed close to 2,000 movies during my years as a film critic. I also wrote a regular weekly column of movie news, previews, and commentary, missing *one* week in 19 years.

Spending a workday afternoon seeing a movie in an empty art house cinema wasn't the worst way to invest one's time (unless the movie was a stinker), and, as a confirmed night owl, going after hours to local megaplexes to get private late-night screenings of a mainstream film opening the next day was a perk not everyone gets to experience. Still, it was work, make no mistake.

Monster work weeks arrived when there was a production company doing a shoot *and* a big film festival in town at the same time. In addition to your normal 50-hour work week, *not* including all the work the film and book beats necessitated at home, you were expected to be in three places at once. It was insane, and exhausting, especially when the film festival—Hunter Todd's five-year run with WorldFest-Charleston in the mid-'90s comes to mind—also meant coordinating the work of five or six other reporters and freelancers on top of everything else.

But, hey, that was the job, and I enjoyed it. As I said before, it beat hell out of covering sewer district news. I was also lucky to be covering movies during the period I did. Much has been written and said about the dynamic, innovative energies of the 1960s and 1970s, but the 25-year period between 1985-2010 was no less fertile, and perhaps more so.

The mid-'90s, in particular, saw the flowering of the American independent cinema and dramatic growth in the number of U.S. art house theaters. In turn, these developments heightened American appreciation of international filmmaking to a degree not seen since the heady days of Italian Neo-Realism, the French New Wave, German Expressionism and the post-war Japanese cinema.

Hollywood no longer dominated. The independent cinema guaranteed more diverse, thoughtful and measured work, and would take risks those seeking big box office dared not. As independent film director David Veloz put it so succinctly, "The broader the audience you try to reach, the more diluted and homogenized the message."

People on the outside told me I had a devoted readership, though I doubted the alleged size of it. And I generally took both fulsome praise and rancorous attacks with a boulder of salt, knowing some readers just did not get it, were kind yet overly impressed, or had their agendas.

But one note I received really mattered to me. It was from Elliott Freemont-Smith, a literary critic for the *New York Times* who chanced to read several of my reviews after moving to Charleston and wrote to compliment me as "a genuine critic, not merely a reviewer." That meant something coming from a colleague of his caliber. And it told me that at least someone was noticing.

Thoughts on the
Art and Craft of Criticism

O lucky man, to have had the editorial freedom and autonomy I did. And to participate in the literary and motion picture conversation.

In conducting book and film coverage I always believed I was writing for an intelligent general audience, not the sixth-grade level so many editors insisted was the average newspaper readership. At the same time, I knew that talking down to people was a non-starter. Writing for a literary or motion picture journal was one thing; writing for a newspaper more of a balancing act between knowledge, discernment, and accessibility.

What surprised me was how department editors respected the division between straight news and the singular craft of criticism, which required a certain frame of mind and a willingness to fight for standards and go against the grain. I benefitted enormously from minimal oversight. After a period of proving myself, my editor simply left me to do my job without interference. I like to think the attitude was, "He knows what's he's doing. Readers like it. Leave him alone."

I knew that critical faculties had to be developed, deepened, and honed over time. One's tastes had to be broadened and refined (without being over-refined). A certain native skepticism was invaluable, as were a sense of proportion, an understanding of the arts one wrote about, and an insistence on quality.

I had always been a movie buff. And while I enjoyed books, I didn't have the patience to sit and read for long stretches. It was not until much later that books and reading became a passionate attachment. Today, to paraphrase Jorge Luis Borges, I cannot sleep or think lest I am surrounded by books.

Of course, being a book review editor and book critic meant more than researching and ordering books, recruiting and cultivating reviewers, dealing with publishers, and writing reviews of my own. It also meant doing hundreds of interviews with writers. One of the most enjoyable aspects of the job, as with being a film critic, was the opportunity to meet and converse with so many gifted and perceptive people.

Having the good fortune of covering books *and* film simultaneously was a decided advantage, considering how often the movie industry turns to literature for fodder. There was so much interplay between the two that my expertise in one also informed the other, and vice versa. I've always held that a competent reviewer, whatever the art form, relates his or her field to the other arts and to the world from which they are drawn. Making those connections was always part of the pleasure.

And the fundamental philosophy I brought to the table was very much the same.

As I wrote in *Lightwaves: A Film Critic's Odyssey* (Sojourner Books, 2023), "Even the most modest movie is worthy of craftsmanship. It can be made with care, with intelligence, with a certain interior logic, with wit and with feeling. If filmmakers are ambitious but happen to fall short, I tried to demonstrate how or why (in my view) they failed. Yet I also wanted to praise the attempt. By contrast, it was when a director with all the resources at his or her disposal—hefty budget, good actors, skilled crew—got lazy and served up junk that I got rankled. It's a slap in the face to audiences. It says, in essence, 'You're too stupid or undiscerning to know the difference.'"

I tried my best never to get personal in a review, a critical temptation that afflicts all too many writers in love with their own cleverness, but sometimes I simply could not resist, or hold back.

As Luck Would Have It

Again, from *Lightwaves*:

> "There are times when a skewering is both necessary and cathartic. I tried to avoid the cheap shot, no matter how tempting. The more I could rhapsodize about superb talents turning out memorable films and give empty $200-million heaps of garbage the dismissal they deserved, the longer I maintained my equanimity, and evaded the assumption that all critics are cynical clods."

Naturally, as a critic for a newspaper I was obliged to pay equal attention to mainstream movies, yet savored the latitude I was granted to focus on those films I thought most accomplished or significant, not just the blockbusters. Which meant foreign films and the independent cinema.

The same guidelines I used for movies and reporting on the film production industry applied to reviewing books and publishing, with tweaks here and there.

In 2000, roughly halfway through my tenure as the newspaper's film critic and columnist, I wrote the following: "Few things are as rewarding as writing about something for which you feel passion. Any critic worth his salt (or spleen) first must love the movies. Critics want movies to be the best they can be. We're disappointed when they're not. And it's our job to hold films to a higher standard. For without standards, how do we recognize excellence."

Traditionally, the role of a critic is not to reflect the popular taste, nor to hold it in contempt. One must realize and accept that many, perhaps most, audiences go to movies just to be entertained. There is nothing wrong with that. But there are as many types of motion pictures with as many intents as there are categories and subjects. Personally, as an audience member myself, I prefer films that entertain *and* enlighten. Or provoke.

Yes, it smacks of elitism (no apologies), but the reality is that the mass audience has never been a good barometer of quality; usually it's the reverse. For all the talk about the appeal of the democratization of art, there is nothing 'democratic' about art except the opportunity to produce it. Art cannot be democratized. Works of art—and artists—are not invariably equal.

If I had a pet peeve as a critic, it had little to do with the audience. It was the blurb industry. Almost as bad as "reviewers" who never met a movie they didn't like or the self-consciously cerebral critic whose lofty tastes led to disparaging everything but obtuse art pictures, were the fraudulent "critics," non-existent moviegoers whose manufactured blurbs were routinely used for promotion.

I felt the same way about the rapturous burbs emblazoned on the covers and inside pages of books. While some were doubtless sincere, and a valid reflection of the caliber of a book, many more were grossly exaggerated or mere pats on the back from friends and fellow writers, *quid pro quo*.

Not that my work was faultless. I made plenty of mistakes, some of them bone-headed. I failed to make a connection in something I'd read or watched until after deadline when my review or story was "put to bed" and it was too late to revise it. An example of this, amusing in retrospect, was my review of the movie *Havana*, starring Robert Redford, Lena Olin, and Alan Arkin. Hours after filing my review I had dinner with friends who asked me what I'd seen that day. As I described the plot of the film, I noted that the Redford character was a lot like Humphrey Bogart's in *Casablanca*, that Olin's resembled Ingrid Bergman's in the same film, that Arkin's shared much with Claude Rains's and that…I stopped in mid-sentence. *Havana* was a cloaked but still obvious remake of *Casablanca*, and I had missed it. *Good grief.*

Sometimes, on reflection, I didn't even concur with a film review I had written, with little opportunity to digest what I'd watched before having to sit down and write. In daily journalism, that was the nature of the beast. As with re-reading books at leisure, repeat viewings of a movie almost always summoned additional or modifying impressions, things that one may have missed while feverishly taking notes. Sadly, there was no time to catch those, except after the fact.

I flatter myself by believing that most of the time I was not fooled, that I managed to cut through and expose the hype, though sometimes I got caught up in it, too. Enthusiasm can be a double-edged sword. I didn't even mind when a reader called me to task. In fact, I welcomed it.

As Luck Would Have It

Differing opinions are what makes for horse races. And I never once considered myself the oracle, just another voice in the chorus. I took what I did seriously without taking myself too seriously in the process.

Memory is tinged with sadness when I look back. Though some have managed to soldier on, for some years now newspaper and magazine critics have become a vanishing breed, whether in film, books, art, dance, or theater. These voices that had so enlivened the cultural conversation have been stilled, and discerning readers are the poorer for it.

Bill Thompson

Let us pause for a sardonic chuckle.

Below is a humor column I wrote during my years as book review editor, having seen oceans of bad books come across my desk and wanting to fight back against the tide. Averse to offending anyone, my editors killed it. So now, in retribution, I bring it back to life.

"This book is not to be tossed aside lightly; it is to be hurled against the nearest wall with great force," wrote the incomparable wag Dorothy Parker, delivering a definitive *bon mot*.

When it comes to "instant" political and celebrity books, formulaic fiction, pointless prattles and all the rest of the abominable dregs of publishing, I agree with the sentiment wholeheartedly.

Now don't misunderstand, we all have our guilty pleasures, many of which don't even merit a sheepish look when someone asks, "What're you reading?" They are perfectly acceptable, diverting novels or nonfiction books by capable writers. Just not inspired or noteworthy.

That said, when as many as 500 books are released on a weekly basis, an avalanche that threatens to engulf dilettantes and enthusiasts alike, selectivity is all. And that just covers the actual, hold-it-in-your-hands hardcover or paperback. The old strategies and gambits, such as skimming the text or speed-reading (seldom a satisfying approach) won't work in the face of this onslaught.

No, it's best to cultivate a fail-safe self-defense mechanism, so as not to let bad books gain a toehold on your consciousness. To wit: CIRD (a Capacity For Immediate Rejection and Dismissal). And while the occasional gem may slip through your fingers, think of the benefits! A willingness and ability to assay a book on the basis of its cover alone, while long disparaged, is a vital arrow in your quiver.

Any tome with a hyperventilating plug like "Destined to be a classic" or "The pinnacle of literary genius" should be excommunicated on the spot. Similarly, any book with bare-chested swains named Rudolfo, damsels in diaphanous gowns fleeing Gothic castles, or self-help books that mainly allow "experts" to help themselves to your money.

Others to scorn: Any novel sporting a crude painting of an antebellum Southern mansion on its cover, any book by an author who is said to be "inheriting the mantle" of some past literary luminary, any book that quotes lines from Proust, any "My Life With" book by the wholly unremarkable spouse of someone famous, any memoir by someone under the age of 30, or any book set on a ship or airplane and involving a "disparate collection of people from all walks of life" who together face some perilous situation.

Also, any book of verse by a seven-year-old, any fantasy series that promises to be interminable (like 20 volumes or so), any how-to manual produced by the Army Corps of Engineers, any book that claims to whisk some quasi-controversial thing "out of the closet," any book with a blaring subtitle about how this or that political-cultural-religious persuasion is destroying the fabric of America, and, without fail, any fictional multi-generational saga of a powerful family caught in the gale of some holocaust.

Lastly, any book thick enough to choke a dinosaur or give a normal human being a hernia lifting it off the shelf.

The list goes on and on.

As for those gaudy book jackets with titles that insinuate themselves into your line of sight despite a concerted effort to avert your eyes, be chary. Rapturous blurbs from the author's best chum are highly suspect. Rapturous blurbs of any kind, for that matter. Regard them askance. Take all exultations with a boulder of salt.

Trust me. You'll feel empowered, perhaps even ennobled.

Arts Immersion:
On Being an Arts Writer and Editor

"Art is not a thing. It is a way."—*Elbert Hubbard*

It's been said that any work of art that can be understood is the product of journalism, and although that may smack of self-congratulation, there's truth in it. I tried my best to make the arts explicable—to me as well as the reader. And in that I relied on the articulation of artists themselves. The artist Paul Klee said it well: "The object of painting is not to reflect the visible, but to make visible." That principle can be broadly applied.

That Charleston offers far more in terms of the arts for a city its size is one of the reasons it has become a major international travel destination. Much credit for spurring as renaissance must go to the Spoleto Festival, but numerous individuals and arts groups not only have spurred the city's artistic growth but introduced work of a high caliber.

Being arts editor and the chief arts writer, while also selecting national stories for the dedicated Sunday section, was a bit daunting in the beginning, for reasons I described in this book's introduction. Who am I kidding? It was challenging throughout, and not always in a good way.

But I wouldn't trade a minute of it.

Still, I could see the writing on the wall—many colleagues had accepted buyouts or been "downsized"—and I was nearing the day when I would walk away. I had already laid the groundwork, so to speak. I was 47 when I came across Gordon Burgett's *How to Create Your Own Super Second Life*, a workbook for getting the most out of the "extra" 30 years one might get in retirement. I passed it off as just another second-rate self-help book with the characteristically overheated title. I cracked it anyway, if only to see what hackneyed advice the author was purveying. Turns out he was serious, and had taken a sober, comprehensive approach that might actually help people navigate their futures.

As I was nearing the Big 5-0, I had already begun assessing my life to that point as well as my hopes for the future. Burgett helped put some things in perspective, not least the pitfall of just floating through life and never taking charge of it, that the greatest risk to a life well lived lurks in not taking risks.

By age 63, I knew it was almost time to leave the paper. Throughout 2011 I invested much time in studying the fiscal, psychological and emotional issues associated with retirement, and distilled that knowledge and advice into a loose personal strategy. The key bit of wisdom running through it all was to have passions waiting in the wings, which I did. I wasn't done yet, however.

I continued as book editor until my next birthday in August of 2012, turning the reins over to my esteemed colleague Adam Parker, he of the perpetual paper avalanche desk and riotously colored socks. My tenure as a full-time film critic had ended abruptly late in 2009, although I continued, sporadically, to write reviews and film histories through the following year.

Management had decided they needed an arts writer-editor more than a movie maven. After all, they reasoned, the paper was already paying for wire service copy and could get all the reviews they wanted. Short-sighted, in my view, but I understood. The best work I had ever done was being trumped by new realities, like the shrinking newsroom and a heightened emphasis on what was local, local, local (to borrow the real estate mantra).

My experience covering theater, symphonic music, dance, and the visual arts was more limited compared to books and film. But I threw myself into it with the same gusto and sense of responsibility. I had met a great many local artists as a feature writer and had interviewed some of them, as well as a number of national figures. But now I was being immersed in the field fulltime, a gig that was both exacting and invigorating.

Taking on this new position coincided with major growth in the arts in the city, especially of theater companies, but actually of all sorts of groups, each of whom clamored for coverage. Growth continues to this day, but with far less space and far fewer bodies to cover it—a deeply regrettable state of affairs. This was happening well before I retired. I never liked saying no, but towards the end of my years in newspapering, I found myself spending a disproportionate amount of my time doing just that, and having to explain why to incredulous "suitors."

One of my best friends at the paper, whose depth of knowledge and skills I always felt were underutilized, was Jack McCray, the classiest of class acts and a walking encyclopedia of jazz (and basketball) history. Along with Adam Parker, who knew a great deal about symphonic music, Jack was a frequent sounding board as I was compiling coverage. I mention him not only because he was a friend and associate, but because he was instrumental in establishing the vital organizations Jazz Artists of Charleston and the Charleston Jazz Initiative as educational forums. He served as front man, together with trumpeter Charleton Singleton, for the Charleston Jazz Orchestra, unquestionably one of the nation's finest.

The CJO has been top drawer from day one, with such artists as Singleton, Quentin Baxter, the late Tommy Gill, Leah Suárez, Mark Sterbank, and current maestro Robert Lewis. It was almost as much a joy to write about them and give them their due as it was to see the orchestra in performance.

And let me not forget that dynamic duo of chanteuses, Ann Caldwell and Quiana Parler. Nor such fine veteran singer-songwriters as Carroll Brown, Peter Kfoury, and Gary Erwin.

For years now, I've also enjoyed the musical insights and savvy perspectives, as well as the friendship, of singer-songwriter Hector Qirko, a frequent band mate of my oldest friend, Steve Horton. A man and musician of multiple cultural backgrounds, and an anthropology professor at the College of Charleston, Hector is rather like a modern-day Paladin ("Have Gun, Will Travel") or Indiana Jones: sober academic by day, rocker at night. As gifted as he is amusing, a great conversationalist.

More recently I've had the privilege of getting to know the distinguished violinist Yuriy Bekker, concertmaster, artistic director, and principal pops conductor of the Charleston Symphony Orchestra. This, after years of admiring his artistry, and many more of hearing the CSO.

In the theatrical realm I have been deeply impressed by a number of companies over the years, having a particular regard for PURE Theater, its edgy material, risk-taking casts and founding actor-directors Rodney Rogers and Sharon Graci. But just as remarkable in their own ways were (and are) Julian Wiles' Charleston Stage, Mary Gould's South of Broadway Theater Company, Chris Weatherhead and Clarence Felder's Actors' Theatre of South Carolina, Keely Enright's Village Repertory Company, Threshold Repertory, Theatre 99, and the various incarnations of the Footlight Players. The financial fallout from Covid claimed some of the others, sadly, but their contributions remain.

I admired such dance companies as the Robert Ivey Ballet and Jill Eathorne Bahr's Charleston Ballet Theatre, and perhaps should have apportioned more of my time giving them their fair share of coverage.

Covering the arts, and art specifically, wasn't really that much of a stretch, though my command of its vocabulary was far from comprehensive. Lynne Riding was an especially able guide to the visual arts, and I valued her occasional input. As for the rest, I winged it.

I've been captivated by art since my 20s, if not particularly well-educated in its intricacies and culture, much less the politics involved. But in my travels I have been privileged to explore many of the world's most renowned art museums and galleries on five continents (see addendum).

Charleston's museums and galleries also possess notable strengths. The Gibbes Museum of Art, the (new) Charleston City Gallery, the Halsey Institute of Contemporary Art, Redux Contemporary Art Gallery, the 250-year-old

As Luck Would Have It

Charleston Museum, and a score or more of exceptional private galleries in the historic district each play a role in the city's artistic vitality.

Now and then I've tried my hand at art myself. I have a penchant for found object ("junk") sculpture, shadow box symbolism, and cork constructs. I once joined my friend Nicholas Drake, who reviewed books for me and was a sometimes art critic for the paper, in investing each Wednesday for two years working on a massive, multi-piece combination of diorama and sculpture. It had a science fiction theme—a space city—with the science worked out in detail. Eventually it was showcased at the old Charleston City Gallery inside the Dock Street Theatre, and professionally reviewed. The reviewer missed the point, alas, having completely misinterpreted what she was seeing. The space city was not a sad comment on how "dreadful" life had become on Earth, so depressed that we were compelled to venture into space, but the reverse. Only a healthy, vibrant, exceptionally prosperous culture could invest the trillions in funds required to conceive and build such a structure while still meeting the needs of its citizens on the home planet. Ah, well, we had lived with the project for two years; she hadn't.

Nick had that uncommon meld of scientific acumen and artistic ability, almost equally adept at both. He was also a long-time stalwart of the Piccolo Spoleto Festival volunteer staff and had a radio show on the local NPR station. In my capacity as film and book critic, I was honored to be one of his interviewees years earlier. After fighting diabetes for decades, it finally claimed him. He is well-remembered by many.

Recently I happened upon an intriguing quotation from a book I was reviewing, and it seems apt to offer it here. The critic and thinker John Berger is describing silence as an aspect of beauty and one of the most important things about some masterpieces of European visual art. He wrote, "It's as if the painting—absolutely still, soundless—becomes a corridor connecting the moment it represents with the moment at which you are looking at it, and something travels down that corridor at a speed greater than light, throwing into question our way of measuring time itself."

Quite apart from the elegance of that passage, it's what it has to say.

As a one-man gang in day-to-day arts coverage, of the Sunday section fronts five or six articles, most or all were mine. Looking back, I'm amazed I could do all that, plus the book page, plus wading through and editing the wires, etc. I was forced to say "no" to people and explain why far too often. There just wasn't enough time, enough space, enough real interest on the part of management to provide the resources (and extra bodies) to do more, especially when they already had a workhorse on the job. My chief regret from my last two years in the business was how these changes shortchanged the reader.

An Aside: Thoughts on Serving the Reader

While you always want to do well by the people you interview, a reporter is not in the promotional or public relations business. We may rely on each other, journalists and PR folk, but in many respects we're in opposite camps.

A reporter's first responsibility is to the *reader*, not your subject, your newspaper, or your magazine (though try convincing some editors and publishers of that). I confess that there have been interludes when I've stopped what I'm doing and asked no one in particular, "You mean people are actually *reading* this stuff?" with more than a hint of incredulity. You can get divorced from the reality of what you're doing and who you're doing it for amid the hurly-burly of daily newspaper work (less so if you are a news reporter).

But reality always comes back to you, often via a phone call.

I admit it, sometimes I get carried away as a writer: excessive descriptions, too many adjectives, an overly indulged fondness for quotes, etc. I never metaphor I didn't like (thanks, Will Rogers). I've rarely been able to write very effectively in the terse Hemingway style, but neither have I fallen in love with my own writing or my own imperishable wit. *Au contraire*. I firmly believe that dispassionate observers engender trust, the self-involved do not. Not to say you can't spread your wings and have some fun now and then.

When a reporter also is a critic, as I have been, keeping these spheres clearly separated in the reader's mind is vital. Not everybody recognizes the distinctions between a news story, a personal column, and a review.

This, from my book *Art and Craft: 30 Years on the Literary Beat* (University of South Carolina Press, 2015):

> "Articles and profiles may suggest the temperament of the interviewer, and even harbor a veiled comment now and again, usually as connective tissue between the subject's thoughts. But reviews and columns are different animals entirely. The former is about an informed opinion. The latter, an alloy of commentary *and* reportage. Still, many of the pieces which endure the longest are spiced with personality. It's the equilibrium that matters."

Throughout my career I have assumed a newspaper's audience to be more sophisticated than many editors believe, particularly in arts coverage. Ditto for magazines. But I like to think I've avoided "putting on airs." I never considered myself a litterateur, the last word in film criticism or anything else. I was, and am, simply a journalist, bibliophile, film buff, arts lover, avid traveler, and devotee of the printed word.

I believe calcified ideologies lose their intellectual freedom of movement, and that a thoughtful writer or editor should harbor an innate distrust of absolutes and certitude. While a journalist must faithfully reflect an interview subject's individual perceptions and words in an article, it is also the reporter's responsibility to ask tough questions and place matters in context.

You want your signal-to-noise ratio to be high.

Again, it's all about the reader. They expect careful preparation, scrupulous reporting, and unfailing honesty. It's a writer's job to deliver it.

53 Years of Great Conversations
(My Favorite Interviews)

The best interviews are always conversations. It's your goal whenever you sit down with a subject or dial a telephone, and it's why you prepare as much as possible beforehand.

Interviewers need to do their homework and craft intelligent questions as a matter of course, but especially when talking to those whose fame or accomplishments means they've been interviewed many times, have heard every hackneyed query in the book, and have minimal patience with amateurs.

Ask a clichéd question and get a clichéd answer, or worse.

It's about respect, among other things, but never fawning. Leave that to the gofers and yes men and human remoras who cling to the stars, whatever their field.

It would be hard for me to name my favorite interviews with sports figures since I was usually working on a tight deadline, had minimal time with the subject (with rare exceptions) and typically kept things pretty basic. Mostly it was scripted answers to scripted questions, a la "Bull Durham."

This is not to say that the stereotype of the "dumb jock" is a valid one. Many of the athletes and coaches I interviewed were highly intelligent and well-spoken. Some of the older players I'd even call cultured, their off-the-field personalities and sensibilities quite in contrast to the striving of the playing field or court. Monosyllabic answers in the post-game locker room were a kind of protective coloring.

The book and film industries were quite different, as were the fields of music, theater, dance, and the rest of the arts. Since people tend to ask me about movie stars more than others I've interviewed, I'll start with them. But the focus here is not necessarily on the most famous ones (for my exercise in name-dropping, see the addenda).

Often the most interesting actor interviews were not conducted with them during their heyday of popularity or critical regard—when, admittedly, it was much harder to get the interview—but when they had morphed into writers and were composing their memoirs, with or without ghostwriters. They had had decades to reflect on their lives and careers and were often less guarded about their image and privacy, having decided to be more candid (and sell more books). Some interviews of this sort that stand out for me were with Leslie Caron, Robert Wagner, Hal Holbrook, who were all well into their late 60s, 70s and 80s at the time.

The binding thread: professionalism.

The Filmmakers

BORN IN SUBURBAN PARIS, **LESLIE Claire Margaret Caron** developed into a ballerina with very much the same gamine appeal that helped make Audrey Hepburn a star. She made a huge splash with her first film, Vincente Minnelli's *An American in Paris* (1951) starring alongside her mentor, Gene Kelly. After that auspicious beginning, and an Oscar-nominated leading part in *Lili* (1953), she played opposite some of Hollywood's biggest male stars, Cary Grant and Fred Astaire among them.

She enjoyed a second smash hit with *Gigi* (1958), though it was beginning to become obvious that she risked getting typed as an elfin, light leading lady, and some still doubted she had the chops to play more serious roles. That was put to rest in 1962 with a fine dramatic performance in *The L-Shaped Room*, which earned her a second Oscar nomination as Best Actress, a Golden Globe, and a British Academy Award. Caron was physically fearless and a tireless worker, as Kelly had discovered. Yet she was not always easy to cast, and, as she confessed in her memoir *Thank Heaven*, she shared her detractors' doubts.

She was the daughter of a prosperous French father and a somewhat remote American mother, whom she never felt she could please—the main source of her insecurity as an actress.

"I think I did suffer from her lack of encouragement," Caron told me in 2009. "With her, whatever I did, it was all right, but not quite good enough.

I never seemed to reach that point with her. I'm not the only artist to have faced that, of course. It was the opposite of a motivating influence. I needed encouragement and did not get it."

Self-doubt sometimes found her turning down roles she didn't think she was capable of playing, or at least playing as well as she would demand of herself. For she, too, was a perfectionist.

"I kept telling myself I was not really an actress, but a would-be dancer who never quite made it. But I was quite wrong about casting and my capability. It was a lack of faith in myself and a lack of courage. I think I should have been more daring. And I should have learned that more quickly. There is so much I refused because I thought, 'This is out of my range.' I refused a film with Clark Gable if you can believe it. I refused to make 'Les Girls' with the great director George Cukor, and I even refused a film with Gregory Peck. How silly."

Yet when she watched a number of her old movies to prepare for writing the memoir, she was surprised by how well she had done. And her career has had a happy ending. A new generation of audiences have seen her in such pictures as *Le Divorce* and *Chocolat,* and Caron won an Emmy Award in 2007 for her work on TV's *Law & Order: Special Victims Unit.*

Today, at 92, she retains dual citizenship and continues to oversee her hotel in Paris. I wish I could speak to her again. What a classy lady.

☙❧

SINCE THE 1980s, **ROBERT WAGNER** has been better known for his breezy, debonaire work in such television series as *Hart to Hart* and, sadly, for the questions surrounding the death of his wife Natalie Wood, than for his movies.

But he is a singular "bridge" figure in Hollywood, having had one foot in the Old Hollywood of the studio system and another in the modern era. A Michigan native, he moved to Los Angeles with his parents as a teenager and attended the same Beverly Hills High School as did many children of famous actors. Before he knew it, the star-struck youngster was a caddie at the Beverly Hills Country Club, toting bags for a foursome that included Clark Gable, Fred Astaire and Gary Cooper. Several acted as mentors when Wagner aspired to break into show business.

As a young actor he was part of the New Guard of the 1950s and early 1960s, led by James Dean, but Wagner also knew and befriended some of the biggest names of the Old Guard: Grant, Astaire, Spencer Tracy, David Niven, Bette Davis, Frank Sinatra, Laurence Olivier, James Cagney, Robert Mitchum, Noel Coward, and Deborah Kerr.

"Isn't that amazing?" he said to me in a 2008 interview for his book *Pieces of My Heart: A Life*. "To have had the opportunity to have been with all these people and for them to have taken time with me is extraordinary. And also to have worked with some of them. They were responsible for getting me going. They represented father figures in some cases. Some had great caring for me, and I appreciate it so much. I'm so thankful that I was able to recognize the importance of friendship and to carry it with me."

Before (and between) his marriages to the great love of his life, Wood, Wagner dated women as diverse as Debbie Reynolds and Joan Collins, married again, and enjoyed a relationship with Elizabeth Taylor. But one of his more influential experiences was a clandestine four-year love affair—in his early 20s—with Barbara Stanwyck, then in her mid-40s.

As I related in my profile of him, Wagner's amiable image is no pose. In a career spanning 60 years, he has been not only a generous actor on screen, but a consistently gracious and appreciative fellow off camera. In one of the most telling observations in his memoir, he wonders if his ability to sustain a long career has been at least partially the result of his capacity for sustaining long-term relationships.

"That's why I wrote the book, because I wanted to acknowledge all the people who have been kind to me, acknowledged me, and made me aware of what I could do, where I could go," Wagner said. "I've really been so fortunate, and I constantly say to myself what a lucky man I am, because my dream came true."

Despite being a hot young property in his 20s, Wagner would go on to play far more key supporting roles than leading ones in feature films. His most enduring success came with three popular television series: *It Takes a Thief* (opposite Astaire), *Switch* (with Eddie Albert) and the aforementioned *Hart to Hart* (with Stephanie Powers). As many a star actor has learned, good TV is better than bad movies.

Natalie Wood's death in 1981 was ruled accidental, but scandal mongers persisted in suggesting foul play and Wagner's complicity in it. The combination left him a shattered man. His innate optimism and the responsibility of caring for his three daughters helped Wagner recover, as did his later marriage to actress Jill St. John.

When I spoke to him in 2008, Wagner, then 78, was still working.

"As long as I can touch and move an audience, or make them laugh—which is the greatest reward an actor can have—I'll keep going. I always have some projects in the fire."

☙❧

HAROLD ROWE "HAL" HOLBROOK JR. died in 2021, having made an indelible mark as an actor's actor, especially on stage as Mark Twain. I was so disappointed he did not win a richly deserved Supporting Actor Oscar for *Into the Wild* in 2007. Though, I must admit, it was hard to fault Javier Bardem's chilling portrait in *No Country for Old Men*, which won.

It was a sentimental thing in part. I suppose I had hoped Hal would win it in recognition for the body of his work in what was doubtless his last best chance. This, despite the fact that I had long argued against such emotional considerations in selecting the best performances in any given year.

Not that Holbrook lacked recognition. An artist *and* a craftsman, he had won a Tony Award as best actor in 1966 for "Mark Twain Tonight!" a role he had developed while still in college and which he continued to perform as a one-man play for more than 60 years. Holbrook also garnered five Emmys for his work on TV. Yet there was always a feeling that this modest, soft-spoken actor, who died at age 95, deserved more.

Before the 1966 Broadway production, and the now-famous CBS TV special the following year, Holbrook had debuted his signature role Off Broadway as a 34-year-old relative unknown. He recalled being astonished at the immense audience and critical response.

"That 1959 experience was a shock to me," the Ohio-born, Massachusetts-bred Holbrook told me in 2012. "I didn't believe it. I couldn't. How could I have traveled all over this country for five and a half years playing this part, rarely having anyone write a grown-up review, and now have all these big-time New York critics fall all over themselves about it? It also scared the hell out of me. I thought, 'If I'm a star, whatever that is, what do I do now?'"

For years, Holbrook and his first wife, Ruby, had been theatrical nomads, a troupe of two who wandered the country in a station wagon, alighting now and again to do summer stock, and accrue a repertoire. Suddenly, he was a hit, on the Great White Way no less, yet no one had a clue who he was. Twain was the star.

"Mark Twain was the success. Nobody had any idea who I was or what I looked like unless they saw me on (the daytime soap) 'The Brighter Day.' I had to start all over again, being careful not to get typed into playing old man roles."

This vignette, arriving near the close of *Harold* (Farrar, Straus & Giroux), a candid, first installment in Holbrook's new memoir, belongs more properly to Volume Two, *Second Chance*, which, despite being 500 pages into the writing, he never completed.

At 86, he was still touring as Twain, for the 57th consecutive year, and struggling with the specter of slowing down.

"The Mark Twain show has become a marker for the way I live my life, really," he confided. "The engine that drove me as a child is still operating very strongly: to go forward, to achieve, to do my best. I don't give up. And I don't give up on Twain, on going out and doing material of his that is not easy for some people to take, even today, like the cleavage between rich and poor.

"Twain faced that social issue and many more in the latter part of the 19th century and the first 10 years of the 1900s. Most people don't realize that Twain also addressed slavery, racism, religion, politics and women's rights. There is almost nothing on which he didn't touch. I toured the South with the show during a volatile period in the 1950s and early '60s, and if I hadn't been wearing the white suit and a wig as Twain, I might not have made it."

His Twain was a characterization, of course, yet Holbrook told me it hadn't felt that way on stage for a long time. On "the boards" he said things he believed in, things that needed to be said.

"I realize I'm not going to change anybody's mind, but I am interested in talking to everybody, not preaching to the choir."

He retired the role in 2017.

Holbrook made 57 feature films, the last being *Blackway* in 2015. Like Robert Wagner, he seldom played the leading role in movies, but always stood out. Among his best remembered roles were in *All the President's Men* (as Deep Throat), *Magnum Force, Julia, Capricorn One, Wall Street, The Firm, That Evening Sun,* and *Lincoln.*

There were also the top-drawer telefilms like *That Certain Summer* (1972), one of the first movies to depict a gay relationship in sympathetic terms, and *Pueblo* (1973), during whose shoot he lost so much weight to play the part that some feared for his life. Holbrook was the guest star or star of several TV series, most impressively as a U.S. senator in *The Bold Ones.* He never gave less than full value.

Holbrook's autobiography, which chronicled his first 34 years, was dominated by the themes of survival and self-discovery.

"Discovering myself was very difficult because I was always hiding behind these disguises. When I evaluate the first 34 years, it comes down to a single-mindedness about making a living and succeeding, creating some kind of a career you could depend upon. That's a difficult thing to achieve in my business. Even today I don't know what's going to happen in the next six months, except for the Mark Twain dates."

As Luck Would Have It

The roles never stopped coming, as it turned out. It was a talent far too good to waste. And a man far too gracious and thoughtful to ignore.

❧

FOR MANY, **CHARLTON HESTON'S** STAR lost some of its luster not only with time, but with his championing of the NRA and gun ownership. But the man was no gun nut—just a Midwesterner who grew up loving to hunt, seduced by the NRA to be its spokesman. On matters such as civil rights he was on the side of the angels, in action as well as word.

When I first spoke with him, back in 1983, Heston was (reluctantly) embroiled in a public debate with TV star Ed Asner over the principal role of the Screen Actors Guild. Asner said it also had to embrace politics.

So I asked Heston, clumsily, what *he* believed the purpose of SAG was. He answered with exasperation, "To represent the best interests of the actors of film and television, of course!"

It was the one and only time in our two conversations that Heston betrayed anything but patience and openness. He was always thoughtful and courteous, one of the very few actors who ever responded to an article or review of mine with a thank-you note. A true gentleman of the old order. I add him to this section in part because he was the first great star I got to interview. And he didn't disappoint.

Some thought him "wooden" as an actor, despite the mega-star fame born of heroic costume epics. But Heston was better than that. He often got the sensibilities of an age just right, his Cardinal Richelieu in the otherwise campy *The Three Musketeers*, his medieval soldier in *The Warlord* being prime examples. My second chat with him came in 1998, as he was celebrating his half-century in motion pictures.

"My goal in life is to get it perfect, just one time," he told me. He was 74, still a man of undeniable presence, and stumping for his latest book, *Charlton Heston's Hollywood: 50 Years in American Film* (GT Publishing). Heston collaborated with Jean-Pierre Isbouts in writing the book, which explored this enduring star's films in the context of Hollywood's evolution, beginning with his early days as a struggling Broadway actor and his breakthrough in live TV of the late '40s, through to the signature movies— *The Ten Commandments*, *Ben-Hur*, *El Cid* and beyond. Also chronicled, with characteristic modesty, was Heston's public service, including his marches with Martin Luther King, Jr., his tour of Vietnam, his leadership within the Screen Actors Guild and the American Film Institute, as well as his efforts on behalf of film preservation.

What stood out for him?

"You remember, and regard highly, different films for different reasons," he said. "For instance, I'm very proud of the fact that I've made more Shakespearean films than any other American actor, performances on the stage aside. And the fact that I have done more films about significant historical figures—about a dozen, I think—than any American actor I know of. The great men are more interesting than the rest of us, really, and I have had the great good fortune to play presidents and generals, geniuses and tyrants, kings and cardinals. And then I've had my shot to work with any number of great directors and very fine actors and actresses."

The Shakespearean roles mean the most, he said, because they were the best parts.

"These plays are the measuring stick of an actor's work and what I remember and value most of my own work. It's surprising to me that there are so many fine American film actors who never have done a stage play at all, ever. Of the ones that have, almost all have never done Shakespeare, which stuns me."

Heston, who died in 2008, believed he had played more different nationalities than any other American actor, including Anthony Quinn. The most unlikely may have been his Mexican police inspector in Orson Welles's *Touch of Evil*.

"*Touch of Evil* is not a great film; it is unquestionably, however, the finest 'B' movie ever made. One of my main contributions to American film is that I 'bullied' Universal Studios into hiring Orson Welles to direct."

As Luck Would Have It

Heston credited his longevity to an instinct for survival, to the good luck of having worked with great directors and having learned something from each. "Of course, I've also gotten some marvelous parts."

❦

MOST OF THE MOVIE PEOPLE I interviewed over the years were not yet contemplating their memoirs. But they were no less intriguing in many instances.

I would not say **Jodie Foster** was the warmest or friendliest actress I ever met—she's far too private a person to let her hair down with a stranger, especially a journalist, nor has any writer the right to expect it—but she was certainly among the most talented, professional, and intellectual.

I did not have her to myself, as it were. It was a group interview in 2000 on the set of *The Dangerous Lives of Altar Boys,* which she was producing. But things did get off to a lighthearted start with Foster musing about her various career crises. She said she had them every six to eight weeks.

"I run through different things I could do (besides movies). Like, I can do cappuccinos really well. Or, I speak French and I could be a French teacher somewhere. I run through my skills and I think, 'Well, maybe it's not too late.' I think we all have this secret fantasy of doing something that's really meaningful and isn't about someone else's idea of what that meaningful is."

Meaning was mostly irrelevant when Foster began her career at age three in a Coppertone ad, or when she became a sensation as a child actor in the mid-'70s with *Alice Doesn't Live Here Anymore* ('75) and *Taxi Driver* ('76).

Since she was working with a number of child stars in the new film, I was interested in her own experiences as a child actor, as well as her take on what the challenges the youngest actors face today, so I initiated the subject. Foster knew as much or more about the demands and perils as anyone in the business.

"The biggest moment in a child actor's life is when he or she realizes they no longer can play *themselves*," she told us. "It hit me on *Taxi Driver*—like a bolt of lightning. I thought, 'Oh my God, this is what my job is?' I had thought the job was kind of stupid. You know, be yourself and say the lines and when someone told you to do something, you'd do it. I'd played complicated characters before, but without any kind of consciousness at all. It was the first time anyone asked me to play someone that wasn't myself."

Foster said conditions had improved for child and teen actors over the past 15 years (1985-2000). She remembered only too well the ages 14-17, which Foster called the worst years of her life.

"From my perspective I think things are a lot better now, because our culture is better. I do remember some of the horror stories, like being in a commercial and being 4 or 5 years old and having (an adult) actor go, 'Get that kid away from me!' Having directors blaming you for things you didn't do because it was easier to blame the kid. Or being constantly yelled at or just never feeling like you had the option to say no. Our culture's come a long way since then and we're not like that anymore.

"I think that now, if I had to go through it all over again, I don't think I would have gotten through it. I don't think I could go through that pain again. I don't feel that I have the strength to go through it. The only thing that got me through it before was how unconscious I was. You just took one step in front of the other without knowing where you're heading."

Foster thought the new film, an adaptation of the 1994 autobiographical novel by the late Chris Fuhrman about growing up Catholic in Savannah, would appeal greatly to contemporary kids—especially 14- or 15-year-old boys—who would find it refreshing to see a movie that shows their lives in turmoil on the screen.

"It's exciting for me, having been a child actor, too," Foster said. "I love working with kids. Always have. You can't bribe them to do things. You can't make them do things that aren't like them. There's never, or very rarely, alternative motives for their choices, like you get with adults. So for me there's a real purity working with kids."

Foster and her Egg Pictures partner, Peabody Award-winning producer Meg LeFauve, are known for selecting their projects with great care. This one is no different.

"In all the films we make what guides our vision, in some ways, is that we look to do things that are kind of hard, that require a really personal touch," said Foster. "So that means we do less than most people. And I think the films we do usually have a lot to do with our own lives."

Foster admitted that to an extent an actor, director or producer does a movie for selfish reasons, to explore themselves. But she added that the best part is collaborating with a bunch of people who bring in new perspectives.

Not all her roles are worthy of her, though her most recent, 2021's *The Mauritanian,* was a critical if not box office success. But the gravity brought to bear by Foster is unmistakable. She radiates integrity and conviction on screen and off. That conviction has earned her two Academy Awards, three BAFTA Awards, three Golden Globes, and a Screen Actors Guild Award.

Few filmmakers demonstrate such a sense of purpose or such devotion to the collaborative aspects of film. Not to suggest Foster is this oppressively serious person. Her hair-trigger wit and 10-candlepower smile make the actress almost instantly appealing. Steel in a velvet glove? Perhaps. But the steel seems eminently flexible.

☙❧

I THINK ONE OF THE things that made for such an engaging interview with the excellent British character actor **Tom Wilkinson** had to do with the bottles of wine we consumed during a lengthy conversation in his hotel. That, and his unfailing candor.

Sorry, but I must refrain from quoting his comments about a certain actress with whom he had a less than cordial co-starring experience. Happens to every actor, and they usually mask it well.

Fact is, I might not even have gotten the interview in the first place had not his publicist told him a white lie, saying that I'd told her I thought he deserved an Oscar for *The Full Monty.* One of the rare instances in which a publicist took my part.

Wilkinson was in town during the Fall of 1999 shooting *The Patriot* with Mel Gibson and company, but also preparing for a lead role opposite Sissy Spacek in what was to become a superb film adaptation of the novel *In the Bedroom*, for which he *did* receive a Best Actor Oscar nomination, one of five the movie was awarded.

But I had to ask, as an opening salvo, "So, is it true that your role in *The Full Monty* heralds the rebirth of James Cagney, song and dance man?"

His reply was droll. "You can be cruel, you people."

Among the most familiar of British actors to grace the screen, equally adroit at sympathetic or villainous parts, Wilkinson, as 2023 passes the three-quarter mark, remains one of the most in-demand actors in the business.

I've enjoyed his work in almost everything he's done. But his Fennyman, the theater owner and aspiring actor of *Shakespeare in Love,* again displayed his gift for comedy and an ability to embody a character that goes from cynical to sweet in a heartbeat. And it did not require him to do the Hustle.

In *The Patriot,* Wilkinson had a blast playing Revolutionary War-era British Gen. Cornwallis. The only question going in was whether he would have the opportunity to portray a man who was also governor-general of India and viceroy of Ireland, or the Hollywood version.

"What you have to deal with is not the historical character, but the character presented in the script," said Wilkinson, a veteran of the National Theater and Royal Shakespeare Company. "I'm not a great researcher, but I do know a little bit about the character. I didn't want to play him as a villain, and he's written slightly villainously. I wanted to take the edge off that. But of course (a truly historical film) never happens. It's not meant to be a documentary. It's meant for people to go and see it."

Although such brief but comparatively juicy parts as the bristling autocrat he played in *The Ghost and the Darkness* and the ominous academic-spy of *The Ghostwriter* have established Wilkinson's facility for sinister roles, he says doing a sympathetic figure can be more fun, provided he is furnished with complexity.

"Playing baddies is so easy and a little bit dull. Goodness is much more challenging to play. But whatever the part is, it is about professionalism.

As Luck Would Have It

What you get from English actors of my generation is this: They've done a lot and they know what they're doing. They turn up on time, they know their lines, they have an idea of who they're playing and they're cheap. Which makes them very attractive. But that's the least thing you can offer to a director. You should be able to take something that is lackluster on the page and give it something more. That's what you are meant to be as an actor; an actor should an expert."

Wilkinson grew up in Canada, where his parents had emigrated with the dream of forging a successful farm. The roots did not take. The family returned to England and ran a country pub in the early '60s, also unsuccessfully.

"It was then that I realized I would do something else," Wilkinson said, who happened upon acting at age 19 when he was asked to direct a play at school. "I thought, 'I love this so much. I'm good at it.' And that's what I've done ever since. No regrets."

Wilkinson reminded me that for an actor to remain a success is a difficult proposition. He said It depended on what is presented to an actor and at what age it is presented.

"If you are young and a big star is put on your dressing room door, it's difficult to accept several years down the road that the big star is no longer up there. I don't have that problem. The big star is yet to be put on my door, and perhaps it never will be. But that doesn't matter. I do what I do, and I'm comfortable financially. It's given me the most wonderful life I could have possibly dreamt of."

❧

THERE WAS A TIME, NOT so long ago, when writer-director-actor **John Sayles** was *the* great threat of the Independent cinema in America. He remains a leading light, here and abroad, but in his heyday of the 1990s and 2000, he made movies done on a shoestring into an art form all its own. Films like *Lone Star* cemented the respect in which he is held in the industry.

You may disagree with his politics, or find the occasional fit of sermonizing to be objectionable, but if there is one undeniable fact of the career of Sayles it's that he has never sold out. Although Sayles' uncompromising approach has seen him struggle to get his films financed, finding top-drawer actors to star in his films (for scale) seldom has been a problem. Serious actors continue to want to work with him, even if it means passing on a lavish payday.

He called it "carving sculptures out of gravel."

He also confided that, "Because time and film are money, you don't want to do too many takes if you don't have too," he said. "It's important to edit in your head. It's not theater; it doesn't have to be a great or even a complete performance of a scene on the set. It can be made into a great performance in the editing room."

Sayles began as a fiction writer, producing two novels, *Pride of the Bimbos* (1975) and the National Book Award-nominated *Union Dues* (1977), and the short story anthology, *The Anarchist's Convention* (1979). Switching to screenwriting and script doctoring for big mainstream pictures (in part to fund his own movies), Sayles took the plunge in the late '70s. Taking $60,000 in screenwriting income, he directed his first feature, *Return of the Secaucus Seven* (1980), which Lawrence Kasdan unashamedly remade as *The Big Chill* (good, but not as good). He followed with *Lianna* (1982), a daring examination of lesbian awakening.

Films of more recent vintage—*Men With Guns* (1998), *Limbo* (1999), *Sunshine State* (2002), *Casa de los Babys* (2003), *Silver City* (2004)—all were well made, with solid performances.

Though Sayles achieves a heightened state of message with infinitely more grace and care than most, there is no ambiguity about point of view in his pointed pictures, He draws full-blooded, three-dimensional people who come alive on the page as well as the screen. Here is a filmmaker who may be said to have created, at once, one of the best family films ever made (*The Secret of Roan Inish*), among the finest police procedurals (*Lone Star*), an altogether unique science-fiction allegory (*Brother from Another Planet*), one of the most trenchant exercises in American film history (*Matewan*), and an anthem for the Sixties generation (*The Return of the Secaucus Seven*).

"A film finding its audience doesn't really concern me now," he said, referring to his film of that moment, *Silver City*. "I believe that it will. One of the things our movie deals with is the way people see the world differently. One of the things that creates drama is not just that characters want different things or think different things, but that they see the world in a totally different way. So you can't expect movies to be received in a uniform perspective."

The loyalty of actors not only from his main troupe, like David Strathairn, but from those who've only worked with him once or twice, means a great deal to Sayles. He soft pedaled, his reputation as the filmmaker who single-handedly resuscitated the independent film movement in the U.S.

To this day, he continues to doctor others' scripts, and there's more in it for him than a big payday As he told me in 2008, "I'm lucky as opposed to most directors that I know, in that I get to work with a lot of other directors Actors get to work with each other, and writers get to work with directors. But directors don't generally have that experience. I've worked for Steven Spielberg, for Ron Howard, Rob Reiner and a long list of interesting directors."

Unlike those worthies, Sayles said, "Plan B is always to write something cheap to make."

Bill Thompson

The Writers

HERE IS WHERE CHOICES REALLY get difficult. I interviewed close to 500 novelists and nonfiction writers, some multiple times, and I would be very hard pressed to select my favorites, since a great many of these interviews had memorable features. So please forgive me for not having accorded them, and those of other creative disciplines below, the same attention as the actors.

One might assume the late Pat Conroy, the pride of South Carolina, was at the top of the list. And I certainly enjoyed those interviews immensely, especially after he realized that I took matters seriously (and was a fellow basketball enthusiast). He was a special fellow, a gifted writer, and I was gratified that the last few years of his sometimes troubled life were the best, thanks in no small measure to his wife Sandy (a.k.a., author Cassandra King).

I still have the three-volume *A Dance to the Music of Time* by Anthony Powell that Pat gave me in appreciation of my work as a book review editor and supporter of writers and reading. They have pride of place in my bookshelves.

I could write oceans of anecdotes on authors I have known, but it would take up way too much space. Suffice to say that the interviews I chose to include in my book *Art and Craft: 30 Years on the Literary Beat* (more on that later) were *all* my favorite literary conversations. Among these worthies, in no particular order, were Tom Wolfe, Diane Ackerman, Paul Theroux, Joyce Carol Oates, Norman Mailer, Dottie Frank, Dick Cavett, Josephine Humphries, Rick Bragg, Jill McCorkle, James Ellroy (a wild a woolly one), Lee Smith, Edward Albee, Mickey Spillane, Sue Grafton, Carl Hiassen, Dori Sanders, Shelby Foote, Susan Millar Williams, Tim O'Brien, Gary Smith, Lisa Rojak, Bret Lott, Mary Alice Monroe, Michael Cunningham, Harriett McBryde Johnson, Charles Baxter, Nicole Seitz, Jim Hutchisson, Greg Jaynes, Patricia Cornwell, Donald Spoto, Barbara Bellows, Billy Baldwin, David Quammen, Elise Blackwell, Tony Horwitz, R.W. Apple, Edward Ball, Anne Rivers Siddons, Anthony Doerr, Joe Queenan, Carl Reiner, David Steinberg, Harlan Greene, and my great friend Ben Moise.

As Luck Would Have It

Some won my admiration for multiple reasons, and many produced work that are touchstones and pivot points in American letters. Diane Ackerman, in particular, stands out at as a double-threat, a remarkably gifted poet—her 1998 collection *I Praise My Destroyer* being a particular favorite—as well as one of the finest writers on the natural world and the marvel of human senses that has ever been my privilege to meet—and, of course, to read. I don't think any book in my voluminous collection has quite so many bookmarked or dog-eared pages as her magisterial *A Natural History of the Senses* (1990).

During one of our correspondences, she reflected on what she loved most about the physical book, while admitting she also sampled audiobooks:

"I prefer holding a fragrant, vellumy book whose spine I can cup in my hand, whose cover I can press against my chest, with big margins where my thumbs can rest, and pages where I can underline felicitous phrases and images or pause at ideas I want to dwell on. I like portable minds, especially if they seem kindred spirits, and books make endearing companions to sit beside or work among. Also, reading is a wonderful sensory experience, like friendship, and I enjoy spending time with an author. When I listen to an audiobook, the words go by too quickly."

I could not agree more. There is nothing like holding a book, or living in their embrace. A personal library can be among our most enriching possessions. Thy page and thy words, they comfort me.

One more literary anecdote, if I may. For many years I had watched the televised programs of that amusing, incomparable interviewer Dick Cavett, never suspecting that one day I would be interviewing him. I got that opportunity in 2010 with the publication of his memoir *Talk Show: Confrontations, Pointed Commentary, and Off-Screen Secrets* (Times Books). Like many authors, he accepted the fact that many journalists did not have the time (or willingness) to read a writer's entire book before sitting down to an interview.

In defense of fellow journalists everywhere, I sometimes received a book from the publisher two or three days before the scheduled interview, when I already had a mountain of work to keep me busy during the day, and films to watch for review or other books to read at night. But I was able the set the Cavett conversation far enough in advance to read his book word for word, and it was an absolute delight.

He was pleasantly surprised to discover I had read *Talk Show* first page to last. "You did read the book, didn't you!" he said, setting the tone for a genial half-hour.

Arguably, Cavett is the wittiest, most erudite and intelligent interviewer television has ever produced, a notable exception to radio humorist Fred Allen's jibe, "TV is called a medium because nothing it serves is well-done."

Cavett toyed with being an actor and magician, before finding his métier as a comedy writer. He got his foot in the door in the early 1960s providing jokes to Jack Paar, then host of "The Tonight Show," eventually graduating to the post of the show's talent coordinator. By 1963 he was a "Tonight Show" staff writer for Johnny Carson and trying his hand at stand-up in comedy clubs. A year later he was on Merv Griffin's staff, but by 1968 broke through as the most sophisticated talk show host in the land. Too sophisticated for some. But "The Dick Cavett Show" found its audience on ABC (1968-75) and especially PBS (1977-82). The diverse cast of characters who sat opposite him included Orson Welles, Bette Davis, Salvador Dali, Groucho Marx, Sophia Loren, John Lennon, and, most memorably, Richard Burton and Kate Hepburn (who was a distinct challenge).

When we spoke, Cavett also was writing a regular opinion column for *The New York Times*, but he was happy to reminisce about the past. The subject of his own style and voice came up. Cavett admitted that writing for a comic with a strong, singular voice like Paar or Carson was relatively easy, but that learning to express his own voice was a different matter.

"It seemed so strenuous (to develop)," he told me. "At first, it was like someone had given you a sleeping pill. You sit at the typewriter, where you are quick to dash things off in order to survive as a comedy writer. I did it faster than most, which made me unpopular with the older fellows on the staff. But writing in my own voice was more difficult."

Praise be that he persisted.

Many other authors are mentioned in "Who I Interviewed," the first installment of my addenda at the back of the book, but I would be remiss not to mention here those authors I interviewed as a free-lancer for *Kirkus Reviews*, exceptionally fine writers such as David Cannadine, Matthew Stewart, Beverly Gray, Malcolm Gaskill, Alan Lightman, and Catherine Bailey, among others.

What a privilege to convey their thoughts, their art, and experiences to the reader. Ditto for ...

The Musicians

CAN YOU BELIEVE THAT WHEN I was going through my mountains of clips a few years back I came upon an interview with Ray Charles that I didn't even remember? No kidding. That's embarrassing.

But after re-reading the piece, his friendliness and easy manner came alive again on the page. That, and his genuine desire that I might get a good story.

Other musicians who were generous and engaging first minute to last were Southern/country rocker Charlie Daniels, the superb film composer and conductor Jerry Goldsmith, Little Feat pianist and co-founder Bill Payne, former Charleston Jazz Orchestra front man Charlton Singleton (now blowing the horn for the Grammy-winning Ranky Tanky), silky vocalist Leah Suarez, the charming and gifted Charleston Symphony Orchestra concertmaster/violin virtuoso Yuriy Bekker, and above all, the inimitable Hector Qirko, an all-round amazing musician/academic and hale fellow who became, as mentioned earlier, one of my most valued friends.

Hector is one of those rare originals. The College of Charleston anthropology professor, who earned his undergraduate and graduate degrees from the University of Tennessee, approaches music with a similar penchant for study and careful composition. And what a remarkable masala of musical influences!

His father's family were ethnic Greeks who settled in Albania. His mother is from Cuba. His parents were immigrants to New York, but also lived in Venezuela, Colombia, Brazil, Peru, and Mexico. As a result, Qirko has deep immersion in varied cultures and musical forms. But it was in the United States that the musician came into his own.

"I don't think I could have helped being interested in culture," her told me during one of our interviews. "After all, I saw lots of different culturally shaped ways to live and think everywhere I went (including in my own home). And it certainly introduced me to many different ways to make music. Thanks to my mother, music of all kinds was very important in our family life."

Qirko left Northwestern University after two years to play with Lonnie Brooks in Chicago, and in 1985 while a student at Tennessee, formed the HQ Band, a blues group that released five recordings and won numerous honors over the course of 25 years. He moved to Charleston in 2010, a watershed event to which our mutual friend (and frequent Qirko collaborator) Steve Horton tipped me off. Hector and Steve have played in each other's' various bands for many years, not least the Lonesome Coyotes.

When we met, Hector was composing and performing in an area that fell under the very loose categories of "roots" and "Americana" music, though he enjoyed and played all kinds of popular music.

"I'm always looking for music that will move me," he said, "and a lot of it gets added to the pile of influences that, mostly unconsciously, shape how I write and play."

With numerous CDs under his belt, and a wealth of knowledge in other fields, Hector is a delightful companion in conversion. We still get together from time to time for a beer and a gab, and I always enjoy the exchange immensely.

Which leads to …

As Luck Would Have It

Dancers and Choreographers

OF THOSE I HAD THE privilege of interviewing, I have particularly vivid memories of speaking to Rudolph Nureyev, one of the great artists of his age; Robert Ivey, a veteran Broadway dancer turned choreographer and teacher who endlessly gave of himself and inspired so many in Charleston; Moses Pendleton, the mesmerizing maestro of Momix; and most recently, tap dancer extraordinaire Ayodele Casel, who is keeping a wonderful art form alive.

I will never forget the outpouring of love and affection that attended the celebration of Ivey's life and career after his death in 2011. The Sottile Theatre in downtown Charleston had an SRO crowd of more than 800 friends, family, colleagues, and students for this gathering, highlighted by a film chronicling his contributions not only to his community but beyond.

Bob created the Robert Ivey Ballet in 1978, and for 40 years it has been a prime player in the process of Charleston's artistic revitalization, including three decades as a standard bearer for the annual Picco Spoleto Festival. His ballet company also toured more than 20 countries, while winning national awards for its original choreography. By extension, its success also encouraged the birth of other local dance companies.

Although I interviewed Bob on numerous occasions, and asked his counsel on others, I can't say I knew him well. We ran in different circles. And journalists are ill-advised, however tempting, to get too chummy with anyone they write about. In a way, Bob's presence still is felt in the West Ashley home of my dear friend Phyllis Licciardi. She and her husband Frank, both of whom I wrote about earlier, bought Ivey's House when they moved here from Iowa in the early 1980s.

A good segue to ...

Bill Thompson

Artists and Photographers

THE LIST OF THOSE WHO gave me the most insight into their craft, vision, and outlook has to begin with Francesco (Frank) Licciardi, in whose living room or at whose dinner table I listened, laughed and learned times without number. Another interview that developed into a lasting friendship. It was Frank's extraordinary portraits, self-portraits, and stylized work that set me on the path of serious art collecting. Well, as serious as a small city newspaper guy could afford. Examples of his paintings grace my living room. I am fortunate to have these works and to share them with others.

But as I said earlier, Frank's greatest gift was a talent for living, and the zest to fuel it. Both of which were infectious. He could be earthy and profane, amusingly so, but at his core was a rare tenderness and generosity.

"I've always thought I was perfectly abnormal," he told me during out very first conversation. "I can look in the mirror and laugh at what I see and still feel good about it. Life is a strange journey and I can't take it or myself too seriously."

Trained at the American Academy of Art and the Art Institute of Chicago, many of his figurative portraits were composed in an abstract expressionist manner with stunning sensitivity to color and mood. They captured the personality of the subject with more texture and at least as much insight as a straightforward portrait, though Frank excelled at those as well. The timing of the Licciardis' arrival in Charleston could have been more propitious, however. In the 1980s, the prevailing ethic of much of the art community was tourist-driven: the city's famous Rainbow Row of homes, for example, was rendered on canvas so often it became as much a cliché as moonlight and magnolias. There were notable exceptions among artists, of course, but most seemed to hew to a conventional, rather limited approach.

And here comes Frank. A gale of fresh air, a risk-taker, an innovator, and a painter of a very high caliber. At the time, Charleston wasn't ready for such an artist. His work was admired and valued elsewhere more than in his adopted city, and sales reflected it. It was only during the annual Spoleto Festival, when he and Phyllis would rent a storefront on Broad Street and fill it with his large-scale work, that his large-scale paintings did well here—and this largely due to discerning out-of-state art lovers who had come for Spoleto. When Frank died in 1991, Phyllis wrote a lovely, touching biography of her husband, *Keep Smiling At Trouble...The Life of Artist Francesco Licciardi.*

But nothing captures the man better than his own words.

"My work searches. It seeks an unknown quantity or quality. I'm not a cerebral painter. I'm intuitive and an experimenter. Sometimes I can't for the life of me tell you ho I managed to get a particular effect. I've learned to free my mind without alcohol. I had to turn something off to turn something on, another of the paradoxes of art."

Although she has enjoyed more success in Charleston, it was no less a struggle for acceptance in the beginning for Lynne Riding here. But she has persevered, and the reputation the former London fashion illustrator has established as an abstract artist and portrait painter outside Charleston, often in much larger cities, now is recognized within. She has exhibited around the U.S. in prestigious galleries, and has had a number of one-woman shows as well as her group presentations. My one interview with Lynne Riding was only one of the first of 20-plus years of conversations about art.

Today, she continues to (gently) correct my misapprehensions and opens my eyes to avenues of artistic discovery previously obscure to me. More, her love of teaching, which she has done at the College of Charleston, the Charleston Art Institute and currently at the Ashley Hall School, is helping produce new generations of artists and art lovers with a firm foundation.

Other artists who made for unusually engaging afternoons and evenings were Tom Blagden, Mary Edna Fraser, Richard "Duke" Hagerty, David Boatwright, Mary Whyte, William C. Wood, Bob Grenko, Brian Rutenberg, Susan Hull Walker, John Duckworth, and Susan Colwell. Let's also have a shout out to the wonderful parties thrown by Fraser and her husband Dr. John Sperry, as well as those of affable physician-artist Hagerty and his wife Barbara, a talented writer.

Road, Rail and Sky
(On being an avid traveler and travel writer)

One of the reasons I loved traveling is that I got to write about it, usually for the *Post and Courier* but sometimes for magazines. I had been doing it for some years before becoming the de facto travel editor of the Sunday Arts & Travel section in 2010.

I was proud of the work, not only of seeing my own travel stories in print, accompanied by the photos I had taken, but of mining the best pieces available on the wire services or from fellow local writers on travel.

I'm up to 71 published travel stories now. And counting, hopefully.

Aside from business trips underwritten by the newspapers for which I worked, brief annual getaways to see friends, or jaunts to the mountains or the beach, I didn't really begin traveling in earnest until my mid-30s. Oh, there was that trip to Montreal in 1972 with Anne, not long before we broke up, and a few minor sojourns here and there, but it was the mid-'80s that saw me stop living paycheck to paycheck, set some money aside, and finally accrue enough vacation time to make overseas travel and more adventurous domestic trips practical.

I can't say it was a conscious decision, at least not in the beginning, but one of the factors in my not having kids and perpetuating the family name (not to mention my DNA) was my modest income, the enormous cost of raising children, and my overriding desire to see the world. As much of it as I could cram into one lifetime. People do manage both, but it's not easy.

Time and money are at a premium. For me, travel was a priority. It still is.

Yes, there are those who disdain the very idea of travel—the a-mountain-is-a-mountain-is-a-mountain school of thought—and some (like Thoreau) explore a universe in their own backyard. But I never found the first argument very appealing, or convincing.

This is especially true of transformational travel, and of those moments of almost spiritual experience nature can provide. I love exploring the great cities, and have been fascinated and invigorated by them. But the wilderness, or even pockets of the wild, can move me like nothing else on earth.

So often this has been among the trees. I will never forget my first encounters with the coast redwoods of California—a Lilliputian among the Gullivers—the sheer majesty and timelessness of them, the silence and tranquility of their groves; or hiking among the Douglas firs in Washington State and Ireland; the giant sequoias and western red cedars of California; the old growth cypress and water tupelos of South Carolina; the spears of Sitka Spruce at the base of Mount Rainier; the chestnut oaks, eastern hemlocks, and tulip poplars of the Smoky Mountains; the curious wave-like contours of the banyans of southern Florida, the bizarrely beautiful baobabs in South Africa; and, not least, the otherworldly Angel Oak with its tributaries of limbs less than 15 miles from my home.

But as impressive as their sheer immensity in height or girth might be, somehow even more awe-inducing was marveling at the ancient, gnarled bristlecone pines of the Rockies. It is on these summits where one witnesses both the great tenacity and fragility and of life, with the bristlecones and ground-hugging plants surviving the fiercest of weather, even as that onslaught pummels and contorts them.

No less transporting was my first glimpse of the Oregon coast, with nary a human in sight for miles. Or a night on the beach at Ponte Vedra just north of St. Augustine, Florida, buffeted by the scout gusts of a gathering storm offshore, the feeling primordial and ominous. Or on the North Rim of the Grand Canyon, contemplating a grandeur painted by the setting sun. Or the splendor of standing at the meeting of the Atlantic and Indian Oceans at the tip of Africa. Or the exhilaration of walking upon a Patagonian glacier. I could go on.

Before the Covid-19 pandemic struck, putting my foreign travel plans in abeyance, I had had the good fortune to visit 20 countries and many of their greatest cities and rural areas, as well as 47 of the 50 U.S. states and more than 30 national parks in North America and abroad. One of my chief pastimes, apart from museum crawling, is mountain hiking, and I've notched a lot of peaks *outside* the national parks, too.

I realize your average 19-year-old supermodel probably has been to that many countries in a year or two, while it's taken me 30-plus, but it's a matter of being seasoned enough to really get something out of it. That's what I tell myself, anyway.

My favorite journeys? Different places for different reasons, but certainly among the most memorable abroad were Sydney, Melbourne, Cairns, and the Great Barrier Reef, Australia (2019), England, Ireland, Scotland and Wales (2016); Amsterdam, Munich and Prague (2012); Buenos Aires and Patagonia (2010); Kyoto and Nara, Japan (2008); Barcelona, Madrid, Seville, Cordoba and Granada, Spain (2006), South Africa (all over, 2004), Italy (all over, 1996), the Yucatan Peninsula, Mexico (1989); Negril, Jamaica (1984); and my numerous excursions in Canada (Quebec City, Montreal, Vancouver, Banff, et al.)

Domestically? I am an American first, an Easterner second and a Southerner third. But most of my favorite trips over the past 30 years have been to the great cities and wilderness areas of the American West—Montana, Wyoming, Colorado, Oregon, Washington State, Utah, Arizona, California—with a particular affinity for the scale and drama of Pacific Northwest. It speaks to me as few places do. But this is not to forget Adirondack Park and the entire expanse of the Great Smoky Mountains back east. The Everglades and the Caribbean, as well. I've also visited just about all the major cities of the U.S. at one time or another, with just a couple left to see: Phoenix and San Diego.

This is the geographic version of name-dropping, I realize, but I can't help it.

Travelling is also a source of my passion for photography, which owns an emphasis on architecture, wilderness areas, cityscapes, gardens, and street scenes. However, I should add that I am chiefly a point-and-shoot type, far from a professional photographer, with a small talent for composition and finding the good shot to take.

Almost as soon as I left the *Post and Courier* in 2012 I signed up with my friend Chuck Boyd's 21st Century Photo Club. Chuck, an ex-Marine combat photographer, had worked for the *San Diego Union* as well as in the film industry and is a terrific advocate for keeping one's eyes open. At 84, he remains a fun-loving optimist.

Over the last decade I've also enjoyed compiling a photographic history of my life, not only the travel excursions hither and yon, but things in general, especially the Charleston years, which grew out of the arduous but satisfying task of scanning into a computer the thousands of photos in my mother's collection. Being the eldest of her siblings, she was the repository of many bulging boxes of prints, and they were a jumble.

While Mom was one of the most organized people around, she had never gotten around to organizing all these pictures, which dated from the earliest days of photography to Dad's photos from Europe during World War II to all our baby pictures. I put them in chronological order as best I could, using various temporal signposts and touchstones. And, like all of the images I had taken, I composed them into slide shows.

I now have slideshows on many dozens of subjects, maybe 75,000 photos altogether. I think of it as a creative hobby. But I digress. Again.

Over time I developed a personal philosophy of travel. And here it is, in capsule.

Aside: Approaching Travel in the Right Way

As I wrote in an earlier book, *Why Travel? A Way of Being, A Way of Seeing* (Sojourner Books, 2021), the why and how of travel are at least as important as the what or the where. Why are we so attracted to it? How can we make a journey as rewarding as possible?

It took time for me to answer those questions.

I discovered pretty quickly that flexibility and resilience were just as essential as curiosity, an open mind, and a desire to explore new vistas.

Some feel it is more advantageous to focus their energies on one place— a great city, say—and explore it to the full. Others take it a step further, using that city as a hub and venturing out along its spokes—to villages, lakes, national parks, or wilderness areas. Alternately, some travelers prefer to see as many towns and nations as they can cram into the time available, having a wider (if shallower) experience. Naturally, no one says you can't utilize all three strategies. Slow is generally better than fast, but not always. You can make a good case for the reverse as well.

I advocate travel for its own sake. Absolutely. But it is wise to heed the words of the great travel writer Jan Morris, lest it feel like an obligation: "Travel, which was once either a necessity or an adventure, has become very largely a commodity, and from all sides we are persuaded into thinking that it is a social requirement, too."

That approach is counterproductive. Following fashion and keeping up with the Joneses are not worthy reasons to travel. As I write in "Why Travel?", a "Traveler's destination is not so much a place, but a new way of seeing things. Travel is not only about where you go; it's about what you bring back. Human nature being what it is, what a traveler carries back is profoundly influenced by those beliefs and values he or she carries in."

You can't permit caution to trump being open and receptive. Whatever you do, leave preconceptions and cultural biases out of your suitcase. A real traveler does not live in a gated community of the mind, and spending all one's time in the company of people of the same economic class, tastes and political outlook, either at home or on the move, is unnecessarily limiting. You cannot help but meet a wider, deeper cross-section of people when away from home— although one hopes you enjoy a diversity of acquaintances there as well.

Extending to everyone that fundamental global currency: respect. There is no substitute. You'll be surprised what doors it opens, what helping hands grasp yours.

I miss the late Anthony Bourdain, his books and various TV series. Apart from being one hell of an observer, he could also be a first-class jerk, as those who worked for him could attest. But he had hard-earned wisdom, such as this, quoted in 'In the Weeds.': "Travel isn't always pretty. It isn't always comfortable. Sometimes it hurts, it even breaks your heart. But that's okay. The journey changes you; it should change you. It leaves marks on your memory, on your consciousness, on your heart, and on your body. You take something with you. Hopefully, you leave something good behind."

Amen to that. And to achieve these ends, winging it just gets you partway there. Do your homework before you travel.

Research is half (OK, maybe a fourth) of the fun. But choose credible sources of information. While it is prudent to stay abreast of the political climate, health concerns or crime in a place you plan to visit, choose up-to-date travel guides and strong magazine or newspaper reportage over what you hear on TV news. And take U.S. State Department reports with a boulder of salt. You'd be apprehensive about going to Minneapolis or Omaha after reading one of these, much less to Bangkok, Quito or Mozambique.

As for travel blogs websites, the sheer number of them can be daunting, and because even some of the good ones appear and disappear so quickly, too many have a how-to emphasis that risks being obsolete in a matter of months. Find some you trust.

Be flexible, even when it's uncomfortable. It is important to remember that while not every trip is going to be wonderful— things can go sideways, and some experiences are simply unremarkable—even journeys that don't go according to plan can be valuable, perhaps even more so. Most of us have experienced journeys that did not seem especially memorable at the time, but remain with us in unexpected and useful ways.

A word on "adventure":

I love it. I seek it. But I also want to leave as small a carbon footprint as possible. I grew up fascinated with books on exploration and adventure, believing these journeys into the unknown to be fundamentally human and ennobling. However, I came to recognize that matters aren't quite so innocent.

Even those among us least skeptical of the motives behind the thirst for adventure may be persuaded that the real (or at least largely real) story of exploration is a murky soup of obstinacy, romantic delusion, fortitude, avarice, naivete, ruthless exploitation, willful stupidity, remarkable endurance, hypocrisy, credulousness, mendacity, breathtaking incompetence, profligacy with the lives of others, adrenalin addiction, etc. The romantic quest for adventure, the race to be first, and the means of financing, usually resulted in deflecting expeditions from their alleged scientific goals, assuming they had any to begin with—from science to showmanship, "discovery" degraded to a publicity stunt.

Clear-eyed assessments have been made on the subject by a number of respected chroniclers, not least Felipe Fernandez-Armesto in *Pathfinders* and Daniel J. Boorstin in *The Discoverers*.

But don't let this weigh on you too heavily, traveler. I don't suspect you're about to go out raping and pillaging and despoiling the environment.

A word on technologies:

Smartphones and other such devices potentially can be lifesavers, tools for heightened efficiency, finding directions, booking reservations, or getting urgent questions answered quickly and on the fly. Overuse makes them an encumbrance, gadgets that insulate you from experience, keeping you at arm's length not only from the people around you but from the immediate stimuli of your surroundings.

Put down your cell phone for a second. I want to talk to you about it, especially its role as a camera. There is a crossroads between experiencing a travel destination through the senses and attempting to capture it in images. The one can augment the other, but too often travelers wind up enjoying a place second hand. There's always a risk that our enthusiasm for photography can take over. When it does, we can become spectators to our own experience. I've been there, adding an excessive number of photographic notches to my belt. It is a challenge to one's self when visiting a visually amazing place, but it's very, very important to absorb what you're seeing with your own eyes. Be still. Inhabit the moment.

By all means, take photographs. They possess the power to arrest a fleeting moment in time and give memory the added, indelible dimension of a visual record. Months or years removed from a trip, these images can be vivid reminders of the small details. But keep in mind the dictum of the great portrait photographer Yousuf Karsh: "Look and think before opening the shutter. The heart and mind are the true lens of the camera."

Of course, today's smart phones have many features, and for some these features are addictive, quite literally. They can be great tools when used judiciously. But too often I see travelers lost in their view screens, oblivious to the world around them. What a waste. What's so urgent? What, in heaven's name, is so *interesting*? It escapes me.

And sheer escape isn't the best of reasons for travel, either. End of philosophy class. Fluency in other languages is not my strong suit, as I mentioned earlier. But a traveler need not let language be a barrier. Native English speakers, and those who learned the tongue, have a great advantage in this world. English is (with apologies to the French) the *lingua franca* of the age, notwithstanding its great competitors, Spanish and Mandarin.

Except for remote places, if tourism matters, English is spoken. In much of the big round ball on which we live, English is understood, which makes matters infinitely easier for the linguistically-challenged traveler like me. Citizens of Bhutan, say, can't say the same, though they probably speak several languages anyway.

Now, if you do speak a second or even a third language, so much the better. It gives you a far superior chance of establishing a rapport—or at least a conversation—with someone in out of the way or rural places who does not speak English.

"Of all the countries I have visited where English was not the native tongue, it was Japan where I felt most at home," I wrote in *Why Travel?* "Partly this is because in certain important (if not always admirable) aspects contemporary Japanese culture reflects that of America, and it's not just a passion for baseball. Like much of the U.S., Japan is highly industrialized, regimented and fast-paced (save for its ceremonies), with a high degree of urban congestion. As for getting around, eight or ten all-purpose phrases infused with a bit of politesse stood me in good stead.

"Combined with a smile, they will do the same for you. In almost any language."

Lastly, whether experienced or beginner, travelers always will benefit from advance study, networking, and planning. And those preparing to set foot on the path for the first time should embrace the excitement of the new. Recall the old adage, trite but true: A journey begins with a single step.

Bon voyage.

Today: Freelancing for Fun and (a Little) Profit

In the summer of 2012, at age 64 and having announced my retirement, I first thanked my lucky stars that I had not been "let go" or "downsized" by my employer as so many talented people had as newspapers became the Incredible Shrinking Institution.

Maybe it was sheer, blind luck. Or maybe, just maybe (if you'll allow the conceit), it was because I was doing a credible job of managing the equivalent of three or four full-time beats and it would be more costly to replace me than keep me.

Whatever the case, I was finally ready to leave. Mentally, emotionally, and otherwise. I was being asked to do some things I found distasteful—nothing unethical, mind you—just trivial, inane, embarrassing things I felt were beneath my "lofty station" as a senior writer, or any seasoned reporter. The sort of stories you would assign an intern or what we used to call a "cub" reporter. In any case, pop culture was displacing more serious arts, and serious (not pompous) writing about them.

But I bear no grudge. I remain grateful to the *Post and Courier* family, for it is exactly that. If I miss anything, it's the people, the camaraderie of the newsroom, even if the banter I'd grown accustomed to over so many years was becoming an endangered species, the victim of accelerating pressures and overwork for all concerned.

The writing was on the industry's wall several years earlier, of course, and I won't bother going into all the cultural and financial reasons this erosion happened and continues to happen. It's all very sad and unfortunate, though there are a few faint glimmers of new possibilities.

Today, when people ask me how I'm enjoying retirement, I tell them I'm *semi-retired*, and I am enjoying it just fine. It's great for your time to be your own again, to have the freedom and wherewithal to work only as much as you wish and not to have to rely on it to make a living (thank you Social Security, Wall Street, and that pivotal P&C pension!). I've cultivated enough hobbies and interests to keep me going for a long while.

But I also like to keep the little gray cells going (as Hercule Poirot puts it), to meet new people, to take on some small challenges (I'm too lazy for the big ones) and to do what I have been doing all these years—writing. The difference is that I am no longer immersed in the stress bath of daily journalism, can take it at my own pace, and have far more time to read the books I really want to read, among other things.

In September of this year, I celebrated my 53rd anniversary as a journalist, and my 11th as a (part-time) free-lancer. The latter comes as something of a surprise.

During my final weeks at the paper, when I was sending out thank-you letters to so many of the professional and personal acquaintances who had helped facilitate my work over so many years, it was with the intention to give them my regards and tell them who on staff to direct their future "pitches" for coverage. I wasn't soliciting anything but good will.

What I did not expect was that some would respond with offers to write for *them*. At the request of Mary Love Herbert, then editor of *Charleston Style and Design* magazine, I had earlier made some suggestions on possible free-lance writers and editors in the community she might approach. When I retired she offered some work to me, and I happily accepted. That began a working relationship with Mary and her successor Debra Kronowitz that continues to this day. Mary and her husband Charles, both avid travelers and travel bloggers, also became personal friends.

As Luck Would Have It

For 10 years I was CS&D's quarterly columnist and interviewer on the arts. But of late, my role is changing, and I look forward to producing more general-purpose stories in the design field. It's a big, glossy leviathan of a magazine, sort of a cross between *Architectural Digest* and *Vogue*, which means you almost need a crane to lift it.

Similarly, when the nonfiction/managing editor for *Kirkus Reviews*, Eric Liebetrau, moved to Charleston, he emailed me one day at the *Post and Courier* asking if I was looking for reviewers. I was surprised he'd want to, but pleased. He said it was a way for him to get his footprint on Charleston soil. But before too long I told him I was retiring, and he asked me if I'd like to review books for the well-known national online and print publication as well. I jumped at the opportunity, which also offered a chance to do author interviews. I couldn't care less that the reviews did not carry a byline.

That was 11 years ago, and I'm still at it. You couldn't ask for a nicer guy to write for than Eric.

But that 325-word (now 300) limit on review lengths took some getting used to. Though I am by nature an incorrigibly wordy sort, my infrequent stints at straight news writing reminded me of journalism school training in how to write short and succinctly. I even did it on occasion.

One of my favorite laments from newspaper history is the probably bogus anecdote of a reporter whose deadline is imminent screaming at an editor, "But I don't have *time* to write short!" And it's all too true.

But a Kirkus review is a different animal. They are *really* short. Review a book on the history of philosophy in less than 2,000 words? Are you kidding me? That said, it was a good discipline to learn. And I get to write much longer reviews for other outlets like the *Post and Courier* and the *Los Angeles Review of Books* (LARB), which makes *Kirkus'* parsimony of length easier to abide. What *Kirkus* does provide, courtesy of Eric, are some of the best books I've ever read. As I write this, I have done 144 reviews for the outfit, all nonfiction, and save for a vanishingly small number of poor or mediocre tomes, they've all ranged from good to absolutely superb. It's a great gig to have, and I'm grateful for it.

Why only nonfiction, you ask? OK, you didn't ask. But here's the reason anyway. I am a journalist, an observer, with a natural inclination toward nonfiction. It's not that I do not appreciate great short stories and novels, because I do. My shelves are filled with them. I simply prefer to review a wide range of nonfiction because I think there is more to learn. Fiction, with the sometimes exceptions of satire and parody, chiefly is about the human condition—a worthy study. But nonfiction is about that *and everything else* in the universe.

From time to time, someone asks why I don't just try to write fiction. I am not a storyteller in that sense. The overwhelming majority of the fiction writers I've interviewed over the years said it was all they ever wanted to do, going back to childhood. I, on the other hand, had only a fleetingly "romantic" idea about being a novelist, and that didn't even surface until I was 28, when Bill Petry and I tried collaborating on a novel. I had no idea what I was doing, and it showed.

For me, the fiction writing process is unappealing. Story ideas do not occur to me or come to me of a piece like they do to born-to-fiction authors. Fiction is a lonely profession. I am also a short-form writer by inclination, as this undersized autobiography attests. On the other hand, perhaps I have told myself for so long that fiction just isn't in the cards for me that it has become a self-fulfilling prophecy.

Maybe I'll try again one day, as a challenge, but don't hold your breath. Now that my "anecdotage" is setting in, more likely I'll just stick to what I'm already doing.

One interesting (to me, anyway) story from free-lance book coverage actually harks back to my *Post and Courier* days. Most of us who have substantial home libraries also have a quite a number of books we have not yet gotten around to, and it niggles at the back of our minds. Which is not necessarily a bad thing. As David Quammen has written, "Anyone who truly loves books buys more of them than he or she can hope to read in one fleeting lifetime. A good book, resting unopened in its slot on a shelf, full of majestic potentiality, is the most comforting sort of intellectual wallpaper."

As Luck Would Have It

But there are times when you want to peel away that wallpaper and actually read the book. In 2020, I finally drew Wayne Fields' *What the Rivers Knows* from the shelf where it had been residing for 30 years (in various homes) and read it. I was so impressed I found his email address and sent him the following note:

Dear Dr. Fields,

On a sweltering late summer day in 1990, a new memoir arrived in my daily book mail at the Charleston (S.C.) Post and Courier, where for 32 years I served as book review editor. I was immediately intrigued, flouting protocol and setting What the River Knows *aside for personal enjoyment. I was 42, a child of the North Carolina foothills banished to the coast, and, admittedly, a fisherman of no great distinction. Certainly nothing so exalted as fly fishing; spinning reels and cane poles being my skill set.*

But your book and its themes were congenial to me. My intent was to devour it on the spot.

I am chagrined (and deeply embarrassed) to confess that, while I ran a glowing wire service review of the book within the month, my hardcover copy sat on bookshelves in my various homes for three decades, not forgotten so much as waiting its turn, occasionally pulled down with the sincere desire to place it atop my reading list. The fate of the forlorn. It was my good fortune, and curse, to be inundated with books—as many as 30 appearing in the mail each day -- and for one reason or another, What the River Knows *had to endure an unconscionable wait to be read and appreciated.*

And appreciated it has been. A week ago I took a brief hiatus from my reviewing for Kirkus (I retired from daily newspapering in 2012) to enjoy the book it had taken me 30 years to get to. I finished it last night, and I seems to me as fresh as the day it was written.

You feared, modestly, an "awkward fumbling after grace," but gave us prose as lovely and fluid as the arc of a languid cast. Montaigne would be envious.

And what flawless descriptions, metaphors, similes. "Spiderwebs sequined with dew," et al.

I've long had an affinity for rivers and lakes, being a canoeist. And I hiked parts of the Upper Peninsula (Pictured Rocks, in the main) back in 2007, starting in Paradise (are all who visit, like me, cast out?). I only made it as far west as Marquette, regrettably. I wish I had had your book with me at the time, giving my perambulations even greater resonance.

I am going on too long. Permit me to congratulate you on a fine career in letters, which no doubt continues. I hope that your children Sarah and Aaron and Elizabeth have matured into admirable adults, that Karen still enjoys your various eccentricities, that a career in academe became, ultimately, more gratifying for you, and that you finally apprehended (and released) the monster trout that so long eluded you.

Thank you for the gift of this book, however belatedly. It now goes back on the shelf, keeping close company with such favorites as Lewis Thomas, Diane Ackerman, Oliver Sacks and David Quammen.

Its beauty, its questing, its wisdom, will be revisited.

Regards, Bill Thompson

We were at the height of the Covid pandemic, and Field replied to say the missive came to him at a propitious moment, a pick-me-up amid an anxious time. Fields, who had retired from his long-held academic post, was starting on a new book, and I hope my note gave him some additional encouragement. Though I have not made a habit of writing to authors to compliment them on their work—some publications forbid contact between reviewers and authors even after a review has run—I have dispatched a note of admiration now and then. Everyone likes a little feedback, even established writers.

It's three years later, and I know my free-lance assignments will never make me rich. You don't do what I do primarily for the money. You do it for the pleasure, for the work, to meet new people, and for a bit of supplemental income. In all candor, I don't think I could have ever made a living as a full-time free-lance writer. It's just too arduous, competitive, and uncertain. Life's too short—unless you're a natural, and are driven to be totally independent as a journalist.

Newspaper journalism was the professional trade-off. As a wage slave for 41 years, I always knew the paycheck would be there in two weeks, that the medical and dental insurance was secure, and that'd I'd get my two to four weeks of paid vacation. I left it to others more suited to the task to worry about the business end.

Publishing Books
(a.k.a., Pulling Teeth)

There have been times while reviewing books or simply reading them for pleasure that I have been so moved, so impressed, even awed by another writer's storytelling gifts or powers of observation that I ask myself, "Why do you even bother?" Writing, that is.

But I get over it. Not everyone can be Shakespeare. Some of us just have to muddle along doing the best we can with what talents we were given and be thankful for that much. As we used to joke (ironically) as poorly paid newspaper reporters, "Hey, we could have had to *work* for a living."

It's a bit embarrassing to admit that I did not publish a book until I was 67 years old. I recall a scene from the wonderful 1940 movie *The Philadelphia Story* when the character played by Kate Hepburn asks the young writer (Jimmy Stewart) how many books he has written. "One," he replies. To which she remarks, "That's not very much for a man of 30."

OK, so I was more than twice that age. In my defense, the Stewart character had not toiled for four decades in high-stress newspapering, writing an average of two to three million words a year. Who had time to write books? Well, many do manage to do so. That I finally did write one had more to do with serendipity than intent, though I had to agree it was high time.

Jonathan Haupt, then editor of the University of South Carolina Press, and now director of the Pat Conroy Literary Center in Beaufort, S.C., approached me shortly after my retirement in 2012 and inquired if I'd like to do a book on my years as a book review editor and book critic. I was flattered, to say the least, but dubious. I refrained from expressing my doubts, but there were many. Who would want to read it? Did it really have an audience? Was anyone even reading reviews anymore? And more to the point, would a book by an unknown writer in a small South Carolina city draw the attention of people outside the state, or even *within*?

True, it might stand as a sort of historical document of a point in time in South Carolina (and U.S.) letters, and yes, I was proud of the material I could present. But I still had to wonder if it was a good idea even for a state-supported publisher which didn't have to worry as much about making a profit.

Long story short, I did the book. Jonathan was pleased with it, and it received good reviews.

Art and Craft: 30 Years on the Literary Beat, a collection of my literary interviews and book reviews, was published in 2015. Like I predicted, however, its sales were less than stellar. I felt bad for USC Press, but what was I to do about it? I had performed the obligatory promotion and interviews—self-sales does not come naturally to me—even getting on Walter Edgar's respected NPR radio show.

My good friend, novelist Dorothea ("Dottie") Benton Frank, advised me not to lose heart, that it was all part of paying my dues as an author. She was right, but in my mind I felt I had already paid 41 years of dues as a writer.

It occurred to me that since any book I might write would fly under the radar anyway, I might as well write it for me, as a keepsake, something I'd never done. That was part of the idea behind my next two books. Like *Art and Craft,* they would be retrospectives on two other areas that had defined my career: travel and film. They would blend previously published work with new thematic essays.

The first, *Why Travel? A Way of Being, a Way of Seeing* (Sojourner Books, 2021), was a collection of my travel writing and thoughts on a philosophy of travel. At least it had the virtue of offering readers some useful advice on ways to approach travelling to get the most out of it, along with some (hopefully) entertaining and informative articles on various enticing places of the world.

I pitched it to Jonathan, but the timing was poor. USC Press was clearing its backlist of travel titles because people just weren't buying them. And that was the problem. Travel publishing had declined by an estimated 70 percent. Why would readers buy a book on the subject when they could get all the information they'd ever need, for free, from the Internet and cable TV?

I had secured an agent, the redoubtable Nancy Barton, though she told me up front she was in the preparatory stages of retiring. With her help I composed an arresting book proposal—a demanding task, that—and set about trying to fan interest without following the advice that one must build a "brand" through 24/7 social media involvement and blogs, acquiring an army of "followers." Conventional wisdom held that a legitimate publisher wouldn't even read your proposal if didn't have as many "camp" followers as Caesar's legions.

I am not a great fan of social media, though I recognize its good points. For me, it is largely a waste of time. And, as I said, I'd already decided I was also going to compose the travel and movie retrospectives books as personal memory books. But I did make one concession. Having never done it before, I created (with the help of Go Daddy) a website, *Sojourner: The Art of Travel.* I used some of the material that would wind up in the book, the best of my travel photography, and a backend portfolio of magazine writings, along with whatever outside kudos I could obtain from generous readers. If I do say so myself, it was one of the more handsomely designed and inviting websites out there. Everyone that saw it said so. I surprised myself, and had fun doing it. Not that the website sold any books.

After a year of futility trying to interest a legit publisher, I thanked Nancy for her efforts and went the self-publishing route, a path I swore I would never take. How many self-published authors had company policy compelled me to say "no" to as a book review editor? Karmic payback? I was encouraged to self-publish by several friends in the industry who advised that I'd at least get the book I wanted if I cut out the middleman. I did. And it's a quality book, if

I do say so myself. It did modestly well in the end, but lost money, of course.

Recently published (as I write this) is a second self-publishing venture, *Lightwaves: A Film Critic's Odyssey*, the third and final book in the retro-triumvirate of my best work. The format is much the same as the previous two books but is of greater length. Like *Art and Craft*, the hardest part about doing the movie book was the process of poring (multiple times) over all the years of writing I had done on the subject, in this case distilling some 2,600-plus pieces down to a more manageable 200.

For those who have not attempted this, it is rather like judging a short story contest, which I have done several times. Say 300 stories have been submitted. The first time through is fairly easy, separating the adept from the beginners, the wheat from the chaff. From that point on, it gets progressively harder, and eventually getting to a final "top 10" means discerning the cream from a bunch of equally skillful work. It's a bitch.

Such was the case with *Lightwaves,* only more so. The book's fate is still to be determined, but I'm proud of it regardless.

Which brings me to this, my fourth book of "celebrating" the past. Much further back, of course. In future think I might be well-advised to start looking forward, to write something new, really new. My interests go well beyond books, film, and travel, after all. I am open to suggestion.

Unless one is an historian, looking back puts most non-fiction authors at an automatic disadvantage in the publishing industry, as much of his or her work can seem dated. Or worse, irrelevant. But *As Luck Would Have It: My Polymath Life* is a different sort of animal—part memoir, part autobiography, part rumination.

A word of advice for those thinking of self-publishing: It's sounds easy. It isn't. First of all, you may take a financial bath. Second, it requires what seems like 10 times more work (and hair-pulling) than publishing traditionally, where all one has to do is write, edit, and make some personal appearances. After the book is written, a self-publishing author must hire some combination of professional proofreaders, copy editors, interior formatters, book cover designers and a distributor. A marketing pro will be instrumental, too, unless you already have those skills. But you had better start on your promotional strategy before you set one word to paper.

Also remember, if you are of a certain age, that navigating the online publishing and distribution systems means learning to employ algorithms designed by tech-savvy 20-somethings for tech-savvy 20-somethings who have grown up knowing only the arcane computer jargon their platforms use.

But if you start the process, close the deal. To thine own self be glue, to paraphrase the Bard. Stick with it!

And always heed this tough love from British social and cultural historian Joe Moran:

> "We write alone, as an act of faith in the power of words to speak to others who are unknown and elsewhere ... for the anonymous humanity that may, at some future point, encounter the evidence of our presence in the world. But the act is the reward. Do not expect applause. You must be willing to keep writing in the absence of any evidence that anyone is reading. And no use complaining, either, since no one asked you to do it in the first place."

A knowledgeable acquaintance with whom I had earlier done an interview, Charleston-based memoir coach Mary Johnston (wordworks.com) suggested to me that my memoir could serve a more admirable purpose than what I was dismissing as a self-congratulatory ego trip. It would be one offering young journalists or authors a road map for the processes of researching, interviewing, organizing, revising, identifying an audience, and developing a voice. As she put it, "the things that every writer needs to understand and master." This would be a true memoir, not an autobiography.

Mary knows her stuff. Her counsel was well-meaning and valid. Yet things are radically different in journalism today. The world I worked in no longer exists. By that, I mean newspapering as I knew it. And the sort of writing I have done all these years is not often like the dominant journalistic form: news writing. The simple declarative sentence and I have always been uneasy companions. Not all of the same rules apply, and shouldn't. Also, critics, books pages, and features departments have all but disappeared. There are few such jobs in newspapering anymore, except at the largest newspapers, and even these are vanishing. Historical perspective and institutional memory have little meaning in newspapering these days. It isn't really taught in journalism school, and most students don't have a clue about the past, or how things were done then. Nor do they care. It is largely irrelevant to their job.

I have nothing especially noteworthy to say about the writing process for newspapers or magazines, about the newsgathering process, or about freelancing that would extend beyond a few pages or that hasn't already been said a million times by accomplished how-to authors. If you need that, below is a list of excellent books on the subject, by people genuinely dedicated to the art of teaching what they know. They are experts.

This book evolved in a different way. And I'm satisfied with the approach I took, even if it winds up being just for me. That said, it would be less than comradely of me not to offer *some* direction after 53 years in the writer's trade.

Before someone can write they must first know how to *read*. Deeply. I can think of few better guides for approaching nonfiction (or fiction) than Joe Moran's *First You Write a Sentence.* Moran, a professor of English and cultural history, believes that by "mastering" the fundamental building block of language—the sentence—we learn not merely about writing, but about everything else. He likens good prose to good poetry, both taking wing on the rhythm, meter, and music of language. Writing at its best is an artisanal craft, requiring meticulous care and execution.

Below are some of the books on writing nonfiction I would suggest, either from personal experience or based on long-term reputation:

As Luck Would Have It

- *The Elements of Style* by William Struck Jr. and E.B. White.
- *On Writing Well* by William K. Zinsser
- *Writing Down the Bones* by Natalie Goldberg
- *Immersion: A Writer's Guide to Going Deep* by Ted Conover
- *The Writing Life* by Annie Dillard
- *The Situation and the Story: The Art of Personal Narrative* by Vivian Gornick
- *To Show and To Tell: The Craft of Literary Nonfiction* by Phillip Lopate

CODA

One of my favorite maxims, and one I try to live by, is "Think critically. Live creatively. Choose freely." I flatter myself by believing I've done that most of the time. At age 75, I hope I've accumulated sufficient experience, and reflected upon it carefully, to parley it into some measure of understanding.

Like most people, I struggle with my weaknesses, and may never conquer them entirely. Too often I remain impatient and quick to anger (though also quick to let it go). I can be a wee bit set in my ways. I still succumb to "going with the flow" too much. I'm sure some regard me as opinionated and argumentative. Although I am under much less stress in retirement and take great pleasure in the small things, I would still like to be more serene.

I've tried my utmost to be honest in this telling, character flaws and peccadilloes notwithstanding. Some things must remain private.

If I had set out to write a true autobiography, a searching one, ideally it would have reflected what the late Barry Lopez achieved in his 2019 memoir *Horizon*, through which he hoped he might "create a narrative that would engage a reader intent on discovering a trajectory in his or her own life, a coherent and meaningful story, at a time in our cultural and biological history when it has become an attractive option to lose faith in the meaning of our lives. At a time when many see little more on the horizon but the suggestion of a dark future."

Looking back, I realize that while I frequently worked very hard in my professional life, it was not always intelligently or wisely, that I have taken the easier (not to say easy) way out, the short cut, too frequently for my own good. Not in the ethical sense, but in the manner of giving full sway to that of which I might have been capable. Some of these failures were due to the inherent constraints of newspaper work, but not all. No, not all.

The harshest assessment of my work might be to say that I spent my career strictly as an observer, a voyeur of the experiences of others and reporting on their accomplishments: the athletes, the writers, the filmmakers and artists, the musicians and businesspeople and all the other achievers in multiple fields—albeit in an attempt to showcase and interpret these achievements for the reader. Some might consider this a second-hand life, but that was the nature of most of the sorts of journalism I did and continue to do. For the most part, I'm proud of what I achieved over the decades.

Still, I wonder what I might have accomplished had I applied myself more consistently, had I been more ambitious—ambitious in the best way: striving not for conventional signposts of success, but for genuine achievement and for meaning. I suppose it is not too late. But too often I have simply been unwilling—call it laziness or weakness of vision—to do what was necessary to produce work of a high caliber, distinguished work. To some extent I may plead the limits of talent and ability.

My accomplishment here, if it can be called that, is much more modest. Writing this little book has been another in a long line of interesting experiences, and one I'm glad I undertook. Even if, as I said at the beginning, no one reads it. Naturally, there are a great many things I did not write about. Many tales are told in confidence, and this is not a confessional. Maybe if it was, I *would* sell a few copies. Ah, well.

What would I like people to say of me, both now and when I'm gone?

That I was a loyal and steadfast friend; a clever, sometimes witty, and creative person who loved these same qualities in others; someone who contributed to the to the artistic, social, and political conversation; who championed the written word; someone who never lost his intellectual curiosity or grew stale; who had a keen sense of humor; who loved the natural world and the great cities both; who gave of himself and tried to help those less fortunate. But also someone who made a virtue out of the maverick impulse, and possessed a disarming touch of mischief. Not a bad legacy.

The question is how to bring this book to a close (addenda, notwithstanding). This is only a summation of my life *so far*, and all in all I'm pretty happy with it. If I've not yet achieved total contentment, at least I'm auditioning for the part. And I certainly hope there is a lot more of life to come (which may require a further addendum or three down the road). But I think I've gone on long enough.

Odd for an old Left-winger (me) to quote a sometimes-jingoistic conservative icon, but I will leave it to the late John Wayne (née, Marion Michael Morrison) to supply some singular wisdom: "Tomorrow is the most important thing in life," he said. "Comes to us at midnight very clean. It's perfect when it arrives and it puts itself in our hands. It hopes we've learned something from yesterday."

Say what you will about *today* being the most important. The Duke was on to something.

Here's to all our tomorrows, yours and mine.

Bill Thompson

ADDENDA

(Closing Notes and Lists)

Addendum A

Awards

From time to time people ask me why none of the award plaques I've received are displayed on my walls at home. Easy. I prefer art and photography to ostentation. I mean no offense to those who proudly display such things. I understand.

But for me, the same holds for other sorts of "accolades" like the bogus "Who's Who" listings and even college diplomas. I've never been much for awards, though I've been bestowed my fair share over the years.

I always felt that awards were beside the point, and I did not want my work to be more about the pursuit of awards recognition than the work itself, as sometimes happens with reporters in extremely competitive environments— what folks at *The Washington Post* used to call "creative tension." Of course, that not only referred to the competition with reporters at rival newspapers for the scoops, but also from within. You knew had better produce and produce consistently, since there was always some ambitious young buck or buckette waiting in the wings to snatch your job.

The pressure from editors to win awards was quite real, if seldom mentioned. Their importance to the Evening Post Inc. was understood, which is why for a long time the winners had to relinquish their awards to the company for display purposes, rather than taking them home. But this was nothing like the pressure in the Big Leagues.

The only value I saw in winning an award was that it might mean heightened job security.

So I won some. I'll leave it at that.

As Luck Would Have It

Interviews I Wish I Could Have Done

So many, however fanciful the idea might be. The wonderfully innovative TV personality Steve Allen beat me to the punch years ago with his public television program "Meeting of Minds," in which character actors impersonated notables from differing centuries convening for a roundtable conversation. Different perspectives, different sensibilities, different politics, different belief systems, but great minds all. If I could choose who to sit down across from, it would be…Aristotle, Voltaire, Hypatia, Ben Franklin, Helen Keller, Baruch Spinoza, Beryl Markham, William Shakespeare, Isaac Newton, Barbara Tuchman, Leonardo DaVinci, Frederick Douglass, Katherine Hepburn, John Muir, Eleanor Roosevelt, Sidney Poitier, Jane Goodall, Albert Einstein, Dorothy Parker, Oscar Wilde, Nellie Bly, Cary Grant, Barbara Stanwyck, Lou Gehrig, Saladin, Sophia Loren, Hannibal, Marie Curie, Aristophanes, Meryl Streep, Mickey Mantle, Glenda Jackson, Jimmy Stewart, Queen Elizabeth I, Marco Polo, Augustus Caesar, Jim Brown, Emily Dickinson, Adali Stevenson, Hedy Lamarr, Lief Erickson, Mark Twain, Eudora Welty, Anton Chekhov, Babe Didrikson Zaharias, Christopher Marlowe, Freya Stark, Thomas Edison, Eliane May, Michel de Montaigne, Imogene Coca, Hammurabi, Averoes, Charles Darwin, Catherine the Great, Euclid, Claude Monet, Michael Faraday, Thomas Jefferson, Gertrude Stein, Enrico Fermi, Jerry West, Oliver Sacks, Hannah Arendt, Katsushika Hokusai, Orson Welles, Clarence Darrow, Rene Descartes, Virgil, Duke Ellington, Buster Keaton, Virginia Wolff, Spencer Tracy, Epicurus, Cyrus the Great, Raymond Chandler, William Sidney Porter (O. Henry), Avicenna, Fred Astaire, Ambrose Bierce, Henry II of England and Suleiman the Magnificent.

Where's my bleepin' time machine?

Addendum A — Interviews

Who I *Did* Interview (a partial list)

FILM, TV and STAGE (D-director, A/D-actor-director, P-producer, W-writer, Cr-critic. Most interivews appeared in newspapers. *means article appeared in a magazine.)

Charlton Heston
Barbra Streisand
Mel Gibson
John Travolta
Jodie Foster
Kevin Costner
Nick Nolte
Bob Hope
Tommy Lee Jones
Hal Holbrook
Lily Tomlin
Vanessa Redgrave
Leslie Caron
Malcolm McDowell
Lynn Redgrave
Raymond Burr
Jeff Daniels
Halle Berry
Michael York
Martin Landau
John Sayles (D)
William Shatner
Robert Wagner
Lasse Hallstrom (D)
James Brolin
Peter Fonda
Rudolph Nureyev
Anthony Minghella (D)
Ray Liotta
Tom Wilkinson
Robert Vaughan
George Kennedy
Robert Wise (D)
Milos Forman (D)
Carl Reiner
Jaye P. Morgan

John DeLancie
Robin Curtis
Jim Laing
Susan Stamberg
Charlayne Hunter-Gault
Elsa Raven
Dennis Hopper
Tom Beringer
Blythe Danner
Natasha Richardson
Amy Adams
Jane Seymour
Amanda Seyfried
Ossie Davis
Ryan Gosling
Jay Leno
Oliver Stone (D)
Kate Nelligan
Tim Conway
Dick Cavett
Nicholas Meyer (W/D)
Will Patton
Ruby Dee
Ray Harryhausen (D)
Victor Nunez (D)
David Steinberg
Virginia Madsen
Kimberly Elise
Mehki Pfeiffer
Bill Plympton (D)
Victoria Jackson
Pat Paulsen
LeVar Burton
James Doohan
George Takei
Pat Hingle

Corin Redgrave
Rachel McAdams
Michael Apted (D)
Maria Bello
Tom Sullivan
Aidan Quinn
Nick Cassavetes (A/D)
Aaron Eckhart
James Marsden
Peter Firth
Danny Aiello
Campbell Scott
Vanna White
Ross McIlwee (D)
Clayton Moore (Lone Ranger)
Julie Dash (D)
Kyle MacLachlan
Tim Blake Nelson (A/D)
Thomas Gibson
Chris Munch (D)
Tony LoBianco
Noble Willingham
Henry Jaglom (D)
Randall Wallace (W/D)
Corbin Bernsen
Nick Searcy
Dakota Fanning
Linus Roache
Tony Bill (A/D)
Leonard Maltin (Cr)
Mark Johnson (P)
Mike Tollin (P)
Vanessa Middleton (D)
Burt Wolf
Simone Griffeth

FILM, TV and STAGE (cont'd)

Daniel MacIvor (W/D)
Rick Bieber (D)
Arthur Kent
Robert MacNeil
Ned Fair (D)
Debra Zimmerman (P/D)
Andrew Chiaramonte (D)
Leigh Murray (P)
Peter Wentworth (P)
Stephen Sommers (D)
Hector Carre (D)
Allie Light (D)
Sue Maxman
John Hopkins (D)
Vanessa White
Dane Krogman (W)
Jason Scott Lee
Dale Rosenblum (D)
Frank Runyeon
Lena Headey
Sunny Abberton (D)
Kevin Meyer (D)
Sam Sheffer (D)
Elizabeth Janeway (D)
Keva Rosenfield (D)
Leon Gast (D)
Dick Estell (radio)
David Rocksavage (D)
Julian Adams (D)
Guillermo Arriaga (W)
Richard Trank (D)
Andy Rooney
Margaret Anne Florence
Sylvia Jefferies
Ray McKinnon (W/D/A)
Andrew Zimmern
Michael Givens (D)
Ken Dalton (P)
Dilana Robichaux
Channing Tatum

John Landis (D)
Steve Rhea (P/LM)
William Borchert (SW)
Drew Fuller
Kim Delaney
Sally Pressman
Gayla Jamison (D)
Casey Anderson
Michael Guillen (P/W)
Nick Locke (ArtD)
Stan Garner (trains)
Carrie Preston
Michael Emerson
Nigel Redden (and *)
Stephen Cone (D)
Martin Glyer
Richard J. Lewis (D)
Laurie Lynd (D)
Lysette Anthony
John A. Davis (D)
Luis Berdejo (D)
James R. Harris
  (playwright)
Harry Shearer (W/D/A)
Peter Sagal (radio)
Mark Claywell (D)
John Barnhardt (P/D)
Richard Wiese
Tom Selington (P)
Moses Pendleton
Rodney Rogers
Benjamin Perez
Kaye Tuckerman
Shanola Hampton
Jeff Howard
Ellen Frick (D)
Matt Czuchry
Kyle Barnette
Maria White
Leslie Vicary

Rachel Wallace
Anthony Lyn (D)
Case Dillard
Mary Morten (D)
Liz Oakley (D)
Ari Pinchot (D)
George Motz (D)
Julian Wiles (D) (&*)
Phil Mills
Gardner Reed
Kelly McDavid
Stan Gill
Marc Platt (P)
Tiffany Haas
Ingrid Craigie
Sharon Graci
Randy Neale
Ryan Phillips (D)
Clarence Felder
Chris Weatherhead
Margaret Ford (SW)
Jake Schreier (D)
Bruce McGill
Joel Gretsch
Alan Stanford (Gate
  Theater)
Mary Gould (P)
Andrew Shea (D)
Jim Holmes (W/P)
David Steen (W/P/A)
Tim Suhrstedt (C)
Will Geiger (W/D)
Ron Richmond (D)
Sidney Bland (SW)
Angela Shelton (SW)
Kevin Smith (D)
Rose Tomlin (SW)
Hal Masonberg (W/D)
John McLaughlin
  (DiveM)

Addendum A – Interviews

FILM, TV and STAGE (cont'd)

Greg Pincus (SW)
Edward Feldman (P)
Steven North (P)
Philip Jackson (D)
Kathryn Erbe
Esther Bell (D)
Daryl Mitchell
Jason Gould
Jeff Poole
Teralyn Tanner
Bolen High (P/D)
Reese Hart (SFX)
Norman Webber (props)
Michael Graham (radio)
Rita Walker

Robert Butler (SD)
Chuck Fallaw (D)
Stefan Forbes (D)
Brittany Robertson
Anthony De Longis
 (A/stunts)
Robert Greenwald (P/D)
Beth Grant
Marcie Marzluff (Th)
George Finnan (Th)
Paul Brown (Th)
*Keely Enright (P/D)
*Vicki Mortimer (set des.)
*Chris Barreca (set des.)

*Juan Ruesga (set design)
*Bill Butler (cinem.)
*Ronald Daise
*Carlie Towne
*Scott Pfeiffer
*Kurt Sprinkles
*Brian Porter (D)
*Irwin Winkler (P/D)
*David Mandell
*Aaron Andrews
*Lara Swallen
*Giovanna De Luca
*Terry Fox (impresario)

WRITERS

Norman Mailer
Tom Wolfe
Joyce Carol Oates
Edward Albee
Anne Rice
Pat Conroy
George Plimpton
Shelby Foote
James Ellroy
Louis L'Amour
Barry Hannah
Carl Hiassen
Lee Smith
Jill McCorkle
John Berendt
Jimmy Carter
Gail Godwin
Billy Collins
David Sedaris
Dick Cavett
Larry Niven
James Patterson

Bobbie Ann Mason
David Rakoff
Paul Theroux
Anthony Doerr
Roy Blount
Michael Shaara
Robert Olen Butler
Doug Marlette
Roger Zelazny
Elizabeth Spencer
Mickey Spillane
Dori Sanders
Blanche Boyd
Diane Ackerman
Tim O'Brien
Kirkpatrick Sale
Padgett Powell
Kevin Phillips
Alan Gurganus
Robert Jordan
 (Jim Rigney)
Cathie Pelletier

Louis Rubin, Jr.
Josephine Humphreys
Dean Koontz
Alan Dean Foster
David Payne
Anne Rivers Siddons
Bret Lott
Lewis Nordan
Valerie Sayers
Sheri Reynolds
Brian Brian Lamb
Randall Wallace
John Lindsay
Sue Grafton
Thomas Keneally
Gary Smith
Michael Malone
William Baldwin
Jerry Bledsoe
Charles Frazier
James McPherson
Edward Ball

WRITERS (cont'd)

John Jakes
Frank McCourt
Homer Hickam
Duval Hecht
Patricia Cornwell
Kathy Reichs
David Poyer
Peter Applebone
Mary Alice Monroe
R.T. MacNeil
Nicholas Sparks
Nora Nora Roberts
Margo Raven
Florence King
Joan Joan Vinge
Gary Chuck Kinder
Jacqueline Mitchard
Erik Larson
Michael Bishop
Jan Burke
Smith Hempstone
Brad Land
Bernard Cornwell
Les Standiford
Paul Hemphill
Harlan Greene
Jim Hutchisson
Jed Perl
Maxine Kumin
Sandra Brown
Kristin Henderson
David Warren
Melinda Camber Porter
James J. Kilpatrick
Dick Côté
Michael Blumenthal
Edwin Yoder
Michael Marano
Alicia Portnoy
Cassandra King

Diane Wakoski
Thomas Tenney
Dorothea Benton Frank
Celia Sandys
James Peterson
Hampton Sides
Robert Morgan
Patricia Kery
Tony Horwitz
Ashley Warlick
Sidney Rittenberg
Jack Bass
Louise Allen
Richard Collin
Robert W. Marks
Catherine Hyde
Jack Weatherford
Philip Lee Williams
Brian Jacques
Sylvia Wilkinson
James Robertson
Marianne Williamson
William Stafford
Jonathan Poston
Christopher Moore
Elizabeth Leland
Martha Severens
James Huston
Callan Pinckney
Matthew Bruccoli
Carrie Allen McCray
Effie Leland Wilder
Christopher Dickey
Barbara Hagerty
Andrew Zimmern
Harriet Keyserling
Alexandra Ripley
Pam Durban
Lee Robinson
R.W. Apple, Jr.

Carolyn Leavitt
Curtis Worthington
James Kilgo
Jack Hitt
David Baldacci
Eli Evans
Lewis Grizzard
Sven Bickerts
Walter F. Murphy
Irene C. Kuhn
Lady Sarah Spencer
  Churchill
Susan Millar Williams
Letitia Baldridge
Gregory Jaynes
Shirley Abbott
Margaret Maron
Emily Whaley
Sara Gilbert
Yusef Komunyakaa
Susan Susan Sully
Wanda Urbanska
Ina Hughs
Robert Robert Rosen
Peter Meinke
Marion Rivers Ravenel
Dale Rosengarten
Stephen Jay Gould
Billy Phil Karesh
Howard Bahr
Peter Golenbock
Richard Bak
James L.W. West
Louise Meriwether
Sara Harrell Banks
Terry Ward Tucker
Charles Baxter
Richard H. Jenrette
Paul Allen
Brian Kelly

Addendum A - Interviews

WRITERS (cont'd)

Jennifer Crusie
Bob Mayer
Mark Ethridge
Barbara Bellows
Max Boot
Joe Queenan
Guilliermo Arriaga
Tom Sullivan
Linda Lear
David Kipen
Joanna Hershon
Katherine Wall
Natasha Tretheway
Larry Doyle
James Rollins
David Steinberg
Robin Cook
Elise Blackwell
Linda Annas Ferguson
Clive Clive Cussler
Ann Rule
Nick Smith
Donald McCaig
Gordon Rhea
John John Ferling
Jack Jack McCray
Suzanne & Craig
   Sheumaker
Bill Bill Geist
Tasha Alexander
Will Allison
Elizabeth Spires
Katie Crouch
Nick Taylor
Rick Bragg
Patti Callahan Henry
Kathleen Parker
Leonard Maltin
Michael Ian Borer
Miles O. Hayes

Jacqueline Michel
T. Lynn Ocean
Thomas Lux
John Thompson
Ken Burger
Anita Shreve
Jon Meacham
David Cox
Simone Elkeles
Scott Turow
Damon Fordham
John P. Avlon
Erik Larson
Nicole Seitz
Jonathan Tropper
Craig Johnson
Jane O'Boyle
Walter Murphy
Nicholas Meyer
Ray McKinnon
Timothy Pauketat
Dacre Stoker
Del Staecker
Rita Mae Brown
Carl Reiner
Brandon Sanderson
Alexander Macauley
Donald Spoto
Heidi Durrow
Carl Naylor
Joseph Wallace
Anne Perry
Ian Johnson
Michael Guillen
Anne Saunders
Philip Leon
Gayle Jamison
Dr. Donald Ryan
Gavin Pretor-Pinney
Curt Weeden

Kathy Pories (ed.)
Nikki Giovanni
Kwame Alexander
Signe Pike
James Swanson
Doug Bostick
Mary Glickman
Brad Taylor
Dan Rasmussen
Herb Frazier
Harriet McLeod
Clint Johnson
Peter Sagal
Matt Matthews
David Quammen
Nan Morrison
Richard Mabey
Gary Nichols
Lisa Rogak
Carol Ann Davis
Lisa Foster
Tami Hoag
Brad Crowther
Thomas McQueeney
Chris Lamb
Sara Arnold
James Longenbach
Isabelle Wilkerson
Tamar Myers
Charles Seabrook
Curtis Worthington
Jon Buchan
Patricia Kery
Nora Rawlinson
   (Publishers Weekly)
Monica Simmons
Chuck Geig
Ruthie Bolton (pen
   name)
Suzanne Cameron Linder

WRITERS (cont'd)

Marilyn Schwartz
Gary Tidwell
Shannon Ravenel
George Orvin
Irene Corbally Kuhn
Andrew Skurka
Robert Black
Margaret Eastman
Anthony Varallov
Daniel Wallace

Janet Turner Hospital
Michael Graham
*James Tobin
*Matthew Stewart
*Alan Lightman
*Sir David Cannadine
*Ronald Daise
*Irwin Winkler
*Malcolm Gaskill
*Catherine Bailey

*Nick Bunker
*Anne Cleveland (CLS)
*Leah Rhyne (CLS)
*Beverly Gray
*Mary Johnston
*Angela Williams
*Dwight McInvaill
*Caroline Palmer
*Adrian Miller
*Wesley Moore

DANCE

Rudolph Nureyev
Robert Ivey
Julie Goell
Michael Wise
Bruce Marks
Linda Haberman
Jill Eathorne Bahr

Renee Jaworski
Julianna Hane
Trudy McIntosh
Michele Wiles
Marina Fridmanovich
Moses Pendleton
   (Momix)

Terence Holland
Jorden Morris
*Lindy Mandradjieff
Sara Bennett
*Kirk Sprinkles
*Ayodele Casel

ART, PHOTOGRAPHY

Francesco Licciardi
Sidney Guberman
Rod Goebel
Andre Harvey
Alex Harris
Georgette Powell
Jack Beal
Mary Edna Fraser
Wolf Kahn
Bill Ravenisi (P)
William Bailey
Richard Hagerty
Tom Blagden (P)
Aaron Chang (P)
Mary Whyte
Vennie Deas Moore
Robert Maniscalco

William C. Wood
Mike Hiester
Brian Rutenberg
Mark Sloan
Sandy Logan (P)
John Folsom
John Duckworth
Bob Grenko
Buff Ross
   (WEB design)
Lesley Wayne
Jim Bishop
Richard Moryl
Rick Rhodes (P)
Charles Parnelle
Joseph Labate (P)
Jill Hooper

Geoff Richardson
Julie Heffernan
David Boatwright
Stacy Pearsall (P)
Susan Colwell
Lynne Riding
Monica Karales
Tom Cross
Susan Powell
Alexander Luke
Virginia Mecklinburg
   (Cur)
Richard Hilton (P)
George Skypeck
Sara Arnold (Cur & *)
Jeremy Lock (P)
*Joseph Burwell

Addendum A – Interviews

ART, PHOTOGRAPHY (cont'd)

*Herb Parker
*Jonathan Green
*Charlotte Hutson-
   Wrenn
*Russell Lord
*Joshua Mann Pailet

*Perry Hurt (conservator)
*Ann Simmons
*Kathy Oda
*Matt Wilson
*Christina Butler
*Susan Hull Walker
*Robb Helmkamp

*Ann & Fernando
   Valaverde
*Jeff Kopish
*Cara Leepson (Redux)
*Wesley Moore
*Sussan Sanavandi

MUSICIANS, SINGERS, COMPOSERS

Ray Charles
Van Morrison
Charlie Daniels
Jerry Goldsmith
Bill Payne (Little Feat)
Tom Paxton
Simon Preston
Dennis Locorriere
   (Dr. Hook)
Gary Erwin (&*)
Randall Thompson
Jourdan Urbach
Joseph Flummerfelt
Monica Yunus
   (Met soprano)
Wilfred Delphin
Edwin Romain
Dilana Robichaux
Lindsay Welch
Lara Wilson
Darius Rucker
Danny Leonard
Clay Ross
Richard Moryl

Brad Moranz
Charlton Singleton
David Templeton
Jordan Elum
Hector Qirko
Cheryse McLeod Lewis
Rhiannon Giddens
Lee-Chin Siow
Stephan Berry
Rob Taylor
JoAnn Falletta
Jennifer Moranz
Scott Flaherty
John Cobb
Mike Mancuso
Pam Wiley
Mark O'Connor
Henry Jerome
John Corless
Loonis McGlohon
Linard McCloud
Greg Lowery
Marcy Betzer
Sarah Johnson

Gene Cotton
Patrice Tiedemann
Anima
*Lee Pringle
*Alphonso Brown
*Louis Lortie
*Jason Nichols (CCA)
*Sandra Nikolajevs
*Larry Farber
   (impresario)
*Leah Suarez
*Scott Rush
*Marshall Forrester
*Yuriy Bekker
*Mary Gould
*Rob & Mary Taylor
*Aaron Andrews
*Lara Swallen
*Carroll Brown
*Tracy Bush Traver
*Eddie White (P)
*Peter Kfoury
*Quentin Baxter

As Luck Would Have It

POLITICS / MILITARY

President Jimmy Carter
John Lindsay (NYC Mayor)
Gen. Wm. Westmoreland
Kevin Phillips
Sen. Fritz Hollings

Gen. Claudius Watts
Adm. Stanley Bump
Gen. James A. Grimsley
*Paul Thurmond

SPORTS
(1 = NFL, 2 = NCAA Basketball/NBA, 3 = College Football)

O.J. Simpson (1)
Bill Bradley (2)
John Wooden (Co 2)
Dean Smith (Co 2)
Sonny Jurgensen (1)
Dick Butkus (1)
David Thompson (2)
Al McGuire (Co 2)
John Havlicek (2)
Charley Taylor (1)
Lou Holtz (Co 3)
Bobby Mitchell (1)
Joe Paterno (Co 2)
Bill Walsh (Co 1)
Roman Gabriel (1)
Burt Jones (1)
Larry Brown (1)
Chuck Noll (Co 1)
Don Shula (Co 1)
Chuck Knox (Co 1)
Paul Brown (Co 1)
Sid Gillman (Co 1)
Walter Davis (2)
Vince Dooley (Co. 3)
Pete Rozelle
   (1, commissioner)
Roger Staubach (1)
George Allen (Co 1)
Ted Hendricks (1)
George Blanda (1)
Kenny Stabler (1)

Cliff Branch (1)
Ken Houston (1)
Norm Sloan (Co 2)
Greg Pruitt (1)
Don Coryell (Co 1)
Billy Kilmer (1)
Dan Devine (1)
Bob Lilly (1)
Lydell Mitchell (1)
Mike Curtis (1)
Terry Metcalf (1)
Jerry Smith (1)
George Karl (2)
Ted Marchibroda
   (Co 1)
Elvin Hayes (2)
Fred Williamson (1)
Bob Dandridge (2)
Steve Dils (3)
Chuck Fairbanks
   (Co 1)
Joe Hall (Co 2)
Hugh Durham (Co 2)
Larry O'Brien (commiss. 2)
Joe Theismann (1)
Bob McAdoo (2)
Terry Holland (Co 2)
Jack Pardee (1)
Earl Faison (1)
Bob Boyd (Co 3)

Scooter McCray (2)
Tates Locke (Co 2)
Dan Pastorini (1)
Roy Jefferson (1)
Charlie Waters (1)
Tom Burleson (2)
Bill Walton (2)
Monte Towe (2)
Mo Rivers (2)
Chris Hanburger (1)
Joe Thomas (Co 1)
Mel Renfro (1)
Harold Carmichael (1)
Terry Hanratty (1)
Willie McClendon (3)
Sonny Allen (Co. 2)
Paul Webb (Co 2)
Kevin Grevey (2)
Jay Piccola (2)
Isiah Robertson (1)
Howard Schnellenberger (1)
Len Hauss (1)
Lance Rentzel (1)
Oliver Purnell (2)
Dave Twardzik (2)
Gene Stallings (Co 1)
Jim Hart (2)
Mel Gray (1)
Ron McDole (1)
Don McCauley (1)

154

Addendum A — Interviews

SPORTS (cont'd)

Nelson Munsey (1)
Bill Brundige (1)
Diron Talbert (1)
Ken Mendenhall (1)
Ron Carpenter (1)
Brig Owens (1)
Pat Fischer (1)
Verlon Biggs (1)
John Dutton (1)

Dave Osborn (1)
Bob Tucker (1)
Fred McNeil (1)
Stan White (1)
Willie Burden (3)
John Matusak (1)
Dave Robinson (1)
Marty Domres (1)
Larry Little (1)

Manny Fernandez (1)
Matt Cavanaugh (3)
Mark Mosely (1)
Don McCafferty (Co 1)
Wilson Washington (2)
Ron Anthony (2)
Sidney Lowe (2)
Darrin Nelson (3)
Andy Johnson (1)

Addendum B

Quotes to Live By: Collected Wisdom

"You almost always discover that the book you're writing is not quite the book you set out to write. When you discover that, you solve the problem of the book. No matter how carefully you work a book out, there's always a moment when it jams. You have to find out why it's gone wrong, where it's been wrongly imagined." — Salman Rushdie

Many writers, including some of the most eminently quotable, have disparaged the use of quotes in a manuscript, regarding it as canned wisdom, a lazy wordsmith's means of masking the paucity or inadequacy of his own thoughts. I disagree.

A great quote offers us the gift of aphorism, a concise statement of a principle. And a writer should feel no compunction about borrowing them. In addition to those quotes that have found their way into the main body of this book, below are some of the most trenchant and memorable ones I've collected over the decades. Including, immodestly, a few of my own.

Enjoy. And be edified.

"If you want your life story to be magnificent, then begin by realizing you are the author and every day is a new page." — Mark Houlahan

"You can't do anything about the length of your life, but you can do something about its width and depth." — H.L. Mencken

"The time you have left is a lifetime in itself. Use it well."
— Michael Boiano

"Do not fear death, but rather the unlived life. You don't have to live forever. You just have to live." — Natalie Babbit

"Would I could stand on a busy corner, hat in hand, and beg people to throw me all their wasted hours." — Bernard Berenson

"Everyone is the age of their heart." — Guatemalan proverb

"Most people say that as you get old, you have to give up things. I think you get old because you give up things."
— Senator Theodore Francis Green

"All life is experiment. The more experiments you make, the better."
— Ralph Waldo Emerson

"I want a life that sizzles and pops and makes me laugh out loud. And I don't want to get to the end, or to tomorrow, even, and realize that my life is a collection of meetings and pop cans and errands and receipts and dirty dishes. I want to eat cold tangerines and sing out loud in the car with the windows open and wear pink shoes and stay up all night laughing and paint my walls the exact color of the sky right now. I want to sleep hard on clean white sheets and throw parties and eat ripe tomatoes and read books so good they make me jump up and down, and I want my every day to make God belly laugh, glad that he gave life to someone who loves the gift." — Shauna Niequist, in *Celebrating the Extraordinary Nature of Everyday Life*

Addendum B – Quotes to Live By

"All work and no play is totally missing the point." — Anon.

"There is nothing so beautiful and legitimate as to play the man well and properly, no knowledge so hard to acquire as the knowledge of how to live this life well and naturally; and the most barbarous of our maladies is to despise our being." — Montaigne, in "Of Experience"

"Live the full life of the mind, exhilarated by new ideas, intoxicated by the Romance of the unusual." — Ernest Hemingway

"We are great fools. 'He has spent his life in idleness,' we say; 'I have done nothing today.' What, have you not lived? That is not only the fundamental but the most illustrious of your occupations. 'If I had been placed in a position to manage great affairs, I would have shown what I could do.' Have you been able to think out and manage your own life? You have done the greatest task of all. ... To compose our character is our duty, not to compose books, and to win, not battles and provinces, but order and tranquility in our conduct. Our great and glorious masterpiece is to live appropriately." — Montaigne, in "Of Experience"

"To aim for the highest point is not the only way to climb a mountain."
— *The Living Mountain*, Nan Shepherd

"To find the universal elements enough; to find the air and the water exhilarating; to be refreshed by a morning walk or an evening saunter… to be thrilled by the stars at night; to be elated over a bird's nest or a wildflower in spring — these are some of the rewards of the simple life."
— John Burroughs, Leaf and Tendril

"Every day we should hear at least one little song, read one good poem, see one exquisite picture, and, if possible, speak a few sensible words." — Johann Wolfgang Von Goethe

As Luck Would Have It

"You've gotta dance like there's nobody watching,
Love like you'll never be hurt,
Sing like there's nobody listening,
And live like it's heaven on earth." — William W. Purkey

"The good life starts when you stop wanting a better one."
— Mickey Spillane

"If you are not fully present, you will look around and it will be gone. You will have missed the feel, the aroma, the delicacy and beauty of life. It will seem to be speeding past you. The past is finished. Learn from it and let it go. The future is not even here yet. Plan for it, but do not waste your time worrying about it. Worrying is worthless. When you stop ruminating about what has already happened, when you stop worrying about what might never happen, then you will be in the present moment. Then you will begin to experience joy in life." — Thích Nhất Hạnh

"There can be no happiness if the things we believe in are different from the things we do." — Freya Stark in The Lycian Shore

"The best things in life are nearest: Breath in your nostrils, light in your eyes, flowers at your feet, duties at your hand, the path of right just before you. Then do not grasp at the stars, but do life's plain, common work as it comes, certain that daily duties and daily bread are the sweetest things in life." — Robert Louis Stevenson

"The words you speak become the house you live in." — Hafiz

"Do what you can, with what you have, where you are."
— Theodore Roosevelt

"Experience has finally proved to be a school that trains me to limit my concerns and tolerate my limitations." — Phillip Lopate

"Be who you are and say what you feel, because those who mind don't matter, and those who matter don't mind." — Bernard M. Baruch

Addendum B – Quotes to Live By

"The world will ask you who you are, and if you don't know, the world will tell you." — Carl Jung

"Selfishness is not living your life as you wish. It is asking others to live their lives as you wish." — Oscar Wilde

"Do not indulge in dreams of having what you have not, but reckon up the chief of the blessings you do possess, and then thankfully remember how you would crave for them if they were not yours." — Marcus Aurelius

"It's not the high cost of living that gets us, it's the cost of living high."
— Anon.

"If you have a garden and a library, you have everything you need."
— Cicero

"A garden to walk in and immensity to dream in — what more could he ask? A few flowers at his feet and above him the stars."
— Victor Hugo, *Les Misérables*

"What an infinite pleasure to have such a host of old associates in the house — and new ones, too. ... They are like so many friends sitting there in their stacks, and they have matured or declined along with me ... and if they are often out of date, well, bless their hearts, so am I."
— Jan Morris, on the books in her personal library.

"The most beautiful thing we can experience is the mysterious. It is the source of all true art and science. He to whom the emotion is a stranger, who can no longer pause to wonder and stand wrapped in awe, is as good as dead — his eyes are closed." — Albert Einstein

"In that moment I realize how much I love the little everyday routines of my life, the details that are my life's special pattern, like how in handwoven rugs what really makes them unique are the tiny flaws in the stitching, little gaps and jumps and stutters that can never be reproduced. So many things become beautiful when you really look." — Lauren Oliver

As Luck Would Have It

"I hear and I forget. I see and I remember. I do and I understand."
— Confucius

"At what point in our lives does cynicism take over from instinct? When we stop feeling the softness of rain on our face and start worrying about being wet? ... stop listening to the sounds carried on the wind or the echo of ourselves inside it? Or when we hear the young voice of an activist on the radio and doubt its validity? When do we make that switch from being part of the natural world to being an observer with an assumed right to control it?" — Raynor Winn

"Education is the kindling of a flame, not the filling of a vessel."
— Plutarch

"It ain't what you don't know that's the problem, it's what you think you know that just ain't so." — Mark Twain

"Children, when they're six or seven — they paint, they draw, they write poetry, and they don't question it. But somehow in the process of education we are taught that only the very talented can do these things, so we end up studying their achievements and trying to understand how they did it." —Peter Weir

"Twenty years from now you will be more disappointed by the things you didn't do than by the ones you did do. So throw off the bowlines. Sail away from the safe harbor. Catch the trade winds in your sails. Explore. Dream. Discover." — Mark Twain

"Time is the coin of your life. It is the only coin you have, and only you can determine how it will be spent. Be careful lest you let other people spend it for you." — Carl Sandburg

"It takes a long time to grow young." — Pablo Picasso

"Happiness is not about having what we want, but wanting what we have." — Anon.

Addendum B – Quotes to Live By

"Sooner or later we all discover that the important moments in life are not the advertised ones, not the birthdays, the graduations, the weddings, not the great goals achieved. The real milestones are less prepossessing. They come to the door of memory unannounced, stray dogs that amble in, sniff around a bit and simply never leave. Our lives are measured by these." — Susan B. Anthony

"Pleas'd to look forward, pleas'd to look behind, and count each birthday with a grateful mind. — Alexander Pope

"I miss letters, postcards, aerogrammes — typed or hand-written, arriving with kaleidoscopic stamps, inked with dates and places of origin. They took time and gave weight to words. Often they went out like shared pages from private notebooks, collaborations with the friends and strangers to whom they were sent." — David Mason in "Voices, Places," on correspondence and the elegance of letters.

"If you can't be kind, at least be vague." — Miss Manners (Judith Martin)

"The writing teachers (strict grammarians) had forgotten that every sentence is really a song, the singing of a world into being." — Joe Moran, in "First You Write a Sentence."

"Science proceeds not as an orderly progression of insights and discoveries, but as an often messy confrontation with the complexity of the universe." — John Gribben (2021)

"Utopians are heedless of methods." — J. Rodolfo Wilcock

"Color is to the eye what birdsong is to the ear: a primal communion between ourselves and nature." — Alan Hirshfeld in a review of "Full Spectrum" by Adam Rogers

"When we try to pick out anything by itself, we find it hitched to everything else in the universe." — My First Summer in the Sierra, John Muir

"(Humor) is a useful trade, a worthy calling, that with all its lightness and frivolity it has one serious purpose, one aim, one specialty, and it is constant to it: The deriding of shams, the exposure of pretentious falsities, the laughing of stupid superstitions out of existence; and that whoso is by instinct engaged in this sort of warfare is the natural enemy of royalties, nobilities, privileges and all kindred swindles, and the natural friend of human rights and human liberties." — Mark Twain, 1888.

"If patriotism is love of country, it is a fair inquiry (to ask) how far one can love a country which he has not studied intimately, over which he has not frequently walked, upon which he has not joyously built campfires."
— James P. Taylor

"Ideological certainty easily degenerates into an insistence upon ignorance." — Daniel Patrick Moynihan.

"The most dangerous worldview is the worldview of those who have not yet viewed the world." — Alexander von Humboldt.

"The mountain summit is not yours. Neither is the romantic love, the accomplishment, the dwelling, even your own life. These possessions are not possessions— they pass through you the same as water pouring through fingers or a bird fluttering through a cottage with open windows."
— Tom Zoellner.

"We travel, initially, to lose ourselves, and we travel, next, to find ourselves. We travel to open our hearts and eyes. And we travel, in essence, to become young fools again — to slow time down, get taken in and fall in love once more." — Pico Iyer

Addendum B - Quotes to Live By

"I have learned that peace is not the absence of trial, trouble, or torment but the presence of calm in the midst of them." — Don Meyer

"The truth is rarely pure, and never simple." — Oscar Wilde

"The further society drifts from truth, the more it will hate those who speak it." — George Orwell.

"To ignore the facts does not change the facts." — Andy Rooney.

"The opposite of a correct statement is a false statement, but the opposite of a profound truth may well be another profound truth." — Neils Bohr

"Ethics requires more than a personal account of good and bad, and the freedom to decide either way. It also asks for a basic willingness to approach the world honestly; to develop a passion for truth, instead of comforting deception." — Damon Young, discussing philosopher Iris Murdoch.

"The books that the world calls immoral are books that show the world its own shame." — Oscar Wilde

"When you reread a classic you do not see more in the book than you did before; you see more in you than there was before." — Clifton Fadiman.

"We shall not grow wiser before we learn that much that we have done was very foolish." — F. A. Hayek

"The study of history is a powerful antidote to contemporary arrogance. It is humbling to discover how many of our glib assumptions, which seem to us novel and plausible, have been tested before, not once but many times and in innumerable guises; and discovered to be, at great human cost, wholly false." — Paul Johnson

As Luck Would Have It

"There are no traffic jams along the extra mile." — Roger Staubach

"Silent, solitary hiking is practically religious. Once you're into it and tired, your thoughts gradually replace the world, and you become a transcendentalist." — Russell Banks

"Life is like arriving late for a movie, having to figure out what was going on without bothering everybody with a lot of questions, and then being unexpectedly called away before you find out how it ends." — Joseph Campbell

"Life is a moderately good play with a badly written third act."
— Cicero

"I am not a lonely person. I love solitude. There's a difference between being alone and being lonely. Writers know that. I have never met a writer who does not crave to be alone. We have to be alone to do what we do."
— Mary Ruefle

"History is that certainty produced at the point where the imperfections of memory meet the inadequacies of documentation." — Julian Barnes in "The Sense of an Ending."

"The more cultivated a person is, the more intelligent, the more repressed, then the more he needs some method of channeling the primitive impulses he's worked so hard to subdue. Otherwise those powerful old forces will mass and strengthen until they are violent enough to break free, more violent for the delay, often strong enough to sweep the will away entirely." — Donna Tartt, The Secret History

"There is a pleasure in the pathless woods,
There is a rapture on the lonely shore,
There is society, where none intrudes,
By the deep sea, and music in its roar:
I love not man the less, but Nature more"

— George Gordon Byron, "Solitude"

Addendum B – Quotes to Live By

"Study nature, love nature, stay close to nature. It will never fail you."
— Frank Lloyd Wright

"If a cluttered desk is the sign of a cluttered mind, what is an empty desk a sign of?" — Eric Klar

"Nothing dollar-able is safe." — John Muir

"You can't have everything. Where would you put it?"
— Steven Wright

"The whole aim of practical politics is to keep the populace alarmed, and hence clamorous to be led to safety, by menacing it with an endless series of hobgoblins, all of them imaginary." — H.L. Mencken

"Growth for its own sake is the philosophy of the cancer cell."
— Edward Abbey

"Man is creation's masterpiece; but who says so?" — Kin Hubbard

"Light travels faster than sound. This is why some people appear bright until you hear them speak." — Alan Dundes

"A conclusion is the place where you get tired thinking."
— Martin Fischer

"The same people who can deny others everything are famous for refusing themselves nothing." — Leigh Hunt

"The empty vessel makes the loudest sound." — Plato

"The world is a comedy to those who think, a tragedy to those who feel." — Horace Walpole

"In art as in lovemaking, heartfelt ineptitude has it appeal and so does heartless skill, but what you want is passionate virtuosity." — John Barth

"With money in your pocket, you are wise and you are handsome and you sing well, too." — Yiddish proverb.

As Luck Would Have It

"Never eat at a place called Mom's; never play cards with a man named Doc; and never go to bed with someone who has more problems than you do." — Nelson Algren

Oh, innocent victims of Cupid
Remember this terse little verse;
To let a fool kiss you is stupid,
To let a kiss fool you is worse.

— E.Y. Harburg

"The best six doctors anywhere,
And no one can deny it,
Are sunshine water, rest and air,
Exercise and diet.
These six will gladly you attend,
If only you are willing.
Your mind they'll ease,
Your will they'll mend,
And charge you not one shilling."

— a nursery rhyme, author unknown.

"It is easier to stay out than to get out." — Mark Twain

"Wherever you go, there you are." — Jon Kabat-Zinn.

"The power of accurate observation is commonly called cynicism, by those who have not got it." — George Bernard Shaw.

"A cynic is a blackguard whose faulty vision sees things as they are, not as they ought to be" — Ambrose Bierce

"What good is the warmth of summer, without the cold of winter to give it sweetness."— John Steinbeck

"Writing is easy. All you do is sit down at a typewriter and open a vein." — Red Smith

Addendum B – Quotes to Live By

"The pleasures of the table are for every man, of every land, and no matter of what place history or society; they can be a part of all our other pleasures and they last the longest, to console us when we have outlived the rest." — Jean Anthelme Brillat-Savarin

"The road to ignorance is paved with good editions." — Anon.

"The human mind is better engaged through imagination than obedience." — Quentin Crisp

"The test of our progress is not whether we add more to the abundance of those who have much; it is whether we provide enough for those who have too little." — Franklin Delano Roosevelt

"Life is a series of inspired follies. The difficulty is to find them to do. Never lose a chance; it doesn't come every day." — George Bernard Shaw

"The hardest thing to explain is the glaringly evident which everybody had decided not to see." — Ayn Rand

"Force and mind are opposites; morality ends where a gun begins."
— Ayn Rand

"There is nothing which has yet been contrived by man by which so much happiness is produced as by a good tavern or inn."
— Samuel Johnson

"It is a mark of the cultured individual that he or she is aware of the fact that equality is an ethical and not a biological principle."
— Ashley Montagu

"Man is not merely the sum of his masks." — Camille Paglia

"Beauty in women and distinction in men are alike in this; they seem to the unthinking a kind of credibility." — Anon.

And if you'll permit me, some originals (I think they are, anyway):

"The problem with having an open mind is that someone's always trying to dump some rubbish into it." — BT

"Prejudice is a foolish limitation on a man's life." — BT

"We Americans didn't invent capitalism and the profit motive, we just carried it to greater and greater depths of avarice, vulgarity and shortsightedness." — BT

"Too often, tradition is just another word for repeating the same mistakes." — BT

"The easiest way to go through life is to believe everything, or nothing. Both free us from the responsibility to think." — BT

"He's the kind of guy whose pockets are as deep as his morals are shallow." — BT

Addendum C

TRAVEL HISTORY (since 1980)

1980	Jacksonville, St. Augustine (Fla.)
1981	Jacksonville; Western North Carolina
1982	Jacksonville; Western North Carolina; Atlanta
1983	England (London, Dover), France (Paris, Angouleme, Jarnac, Cognac, Charente River barge cruise); New York City
1984	Jamaica (Montego Bay, Negril, Ocho Rios); Jacksonville; Western North Carolina
1985	Washington, D.C.; Jacksonville & St. Augustine
1986	Atlanta, Dallas, California (San Francisco, San Jose, Los Gatos, Santa Cruz, Oakland, Berkeley, Lake Tahoe, Squaw Valley), Nevada (Lake Tahoe, Carson City), Columbia, Arlington, Washington D.C., Gloucester (Va.).
1987	New York; Jacksonville; North Carolina
1988	Outer Banks (N.C.); Jacksonville & St. Augustine; North Carolina
1989	Mexico (Cancun, Chichen Itza, Tulum, Isla Mujeres); Jacksonville; North Carolina
1990	Chapel Hill (N.C.); Fort Pierce (Fla.), Fort Lauderdale, the Bahamas (Chub Cay, Nassau, Rose Island, Bimini, Paradise Island); Lake Marion
1991	Boston, Haverhill, Newburyport, Plum Island (Mass.), Maine (Mount Desert Island: Acadia Nat. Park, Bar Harbor, Ogunquit, Booth Bay), New Hampshire (Portsmouth); New York City; Jacksonville; N.C. mountains
1992	Seattle, Mount Rainier National Park, Portland, Columbia River Gorge, Oregon Coast, Redwoods National Park (Calif.), Napa and Sonoma Valleys, San Francisco; Savannah; Folly Beach (vacation rental); Columbia; Asheville, Chimney Rock (N.C.), Great Smoky Mountains National Park (N.C., Tenn.); Jacksonville.
1993	Okefenokee Swamp (Ga.); Boston; Nashville; Jacksonville; Table Rock State Park, Caesar's Head (S.C.); St. Simon's Island (Ga.)
1994	Glacier National Park (Mont.), Waterton National Park (Canada); Washington, D.C., Mather Gorge and Great Falls (Va.); Jacksonville

As Luck Would Have It

1995	Chicago; Washington, D.C., Big Schloss (Va.); Atlanta; Highlands and Cashiers (N.C.)
1996	Italy (Rome, Florence, Venice, Milan, Pisa, Genoa, Assisi, Sorrento, Capri, Stessa; Lake Maggiore & Isola Bella, Verona, Pompeii), Switzerland (Lugano); St. Simon's Island (Ga.); Jacksonville & St. Augustine
1997	Cumberland Island (Ga.) and Jacksonville; The Berkshires (Lenox, Stockbridge, West Stockbridge, Williamstown), Boston, Groton (Conn.)
1998	Colorado (Denver, Rocky Mountain National Park, San Juan Skyway, Silverton, Durango, Colorado Springs & the Garden of the Gods, the Sangre de Cristos, St. Elmo, Bighorn Canyon, San Luis Valley, Aspen, Mesa Verde National Park, Pike's Peak, Box Canyon, etc.); Jacksonville
1999	Washington, D.C.; South Carolina mountains (fall foliage); N.C. Pig Roast; Jacksonville
2000	Seattle, Olympic National Park, Hoa Rainforest, Quinault Rain Forest, the Oregon Coast, Crater Lake National Park, Portland, Columbia River Gorge, Mount St. Helen's National Monument; Hilton Head
2001	Washington, D.C.; Lake Lure (N.C.)
2002	Blue Ridge Parkway (hiking); New York State (Hudson River Valley, the Adirondacks and Adirondack Park including Blue Mountain Lake, Saranac Lake & Lake Placid, Baker Mountain & other hikes; Ausable Chasm, West Point, Lake George, N.Y. & Vermont shores of Lake Champlain, Champlain Islands); Hunting Island (S.C.)
2003	Miami, Miami Beach, Key Largo and John Pennecamp State Park (snorkeling), Key West, Everglades National Park, Washington Oaks Gardens State Park, Jacksonville
2004	South Africa (Capetown, Hout Bay, Cape Point, Camps Bay, Sea Point, Simon Town, Klapmuts, Constancia, Paarl & the Wine Country, Phalaborwa, Blide River Canyon, Kruger National Park, Oliphants Camp, Mopanie Camp, Johannesburg); Memphis (Tenn.); Lake Mattamuskeet National Wildlife Refuge (N.C.) & Cedar Island National Wildlife Refuge (N.C.); Washington, D.C., Alexandria and Arlington, Shenandoah National Park (Va.)
2005	Chattanooga (Tenn.) and North Georgia Highlands; Le Grande Tour: Las Vegas, Zion National Park (Utah), Antelope Canyon & Vermillion Hills Nat. Monument (Ariz.), Horseshoe Bend (Ariz.), Grand Canyon National Park (Ariz.), Death Valley National Park (Calif.), Sequoia National Park (Calif.), King's Canyon National Park (Calif.), Yosemite National Park (Calif.), San Francisco; Santee State Park (S.C.); Jacksonville; Savannah
2006	Spain (Barcelona, Madrid, Seville, Cordoba, Granada); Charlotte; Savannah; Lexington (N.C., 40th High School Reunion), Morrow Mountain State Park (N.C.), Congaree National Park (S.C.)

Addendum C - Travel

2007	Michigan and the Great Lakes (Lake Michigan, Lake Huron, Lake Superior, Traverse City & peninsular wine country, Mackinac Island, the Upper Peninsula & Pictured Rocks National Lakeshore, Sleeping Bear Dunes National Lakeshore); St. Simon's Island (Ga.); Washington, D.C., Virginia countryside & wine country; Savannah; Caesar's Head & Raven Cliff Falls (S.C.)
2008	Japan (Kyoto, Nara, Osaka) and Los Angeles (Hollywood, Beverly Hills, museums, etc.); Kure Beach (N.C., family bash), Gloucester (N.C. 24th Blind Pig Pickin'); Black Mountain (N.C.); Lynches River State Park (S.C.)
2009	Santee Coastal Reserve (S.C.); Providence Canyon and Columbus (Ga.), Jacksonville; Jarrell Family reunion, West Virginia Highlands, Lewisburg (W.Va.), Stone Mountain (N.C.); Beaufort; Poinsett State Park & Manchester State Forest (S.C.); Charlotte and Congaree National Park.
2010	Buenos Aires and Patagonia, Argentina; Beidler Forest (S.C.); Beaufort & Hunting Island (S.C.); Wilmington (N.C.), Gloucester (26th Blind Pig Pickin') N.C., The Outer Banks, Roanoke Island (N.C.), Lake Waccamaw (N.C.); Edisto River tree houses (canoeing).
2011	Jackson (Wyoming), Grand Teton National Park (Wyo.), Yellowstone National Park (Wyo.); Jacksonville (Fla.); Beaufort (S.C.); Charlotte, Gorges State Park (N.C.), Graveyard Fields on the Blue Ridge Parkway (N.C.), Greenville (S.C.); Old Salem and Winston-Salem (N.C.).
2012	Holland (Amsterdam), Germany (Munich) & the Czech Republic (Prague); Le Road Trippe (first trip in "retirement"): Charlotte, Lexington ('64-'65-'66 high school reunion), Raleigh, Wilmington, Gloucester (28th Blind Pig Pickin') N.C., Arlington (Va.), Alexandria (Va.), Washington, D.C., Annapolis (Md.), Newport News (Va.)(Joe & Jeannie Fudge), Wilmington (again), Southport (N.C.), Murrell's Inlet (S.C.).
2013	New Orleans; Montclair (N.J.), New York City, Quebec City, Sainte-Anne, Montmorency Falls Park, L'Ile d'Orleans (Canada); Colleton State Park, Walterboro, Caw Caw Plantation; Folly Beach (S.C., house sitting); Augusta (Ga.); Charlotte (N.C.), Jones Gap State Park (S.C.); Charlotte (again), Crowder's Mountain State Park (N.C.); Savannah.
2014	Greece (Athens, Cape Sounion & Santorini); Santee Coastal Reserve (S.C.); 30th-anniversary Blind Pig Pickin' "The Finale" (Gloucester, N.C.) and Wilmington; West Texas (Guadalupe & Big Bend National Parks) and New Mexico (Carlsbad Caverns National Park).
2015	Trans-Continent Drive & Hike (Minneapolis, Theodore Roosevelt National Park in N.D., eastern Montana, Saskatchewan, Banff/Yoho/Glacier/Mount Revelstoke National Parks (Canada), Kamloops, Vancouver, Vancouver Island & Victoria (Canada), San Juan Islands ferry) and Seattle; Savannah & Tybee Island; Charlotte, Valle Crusis & Blowing Rock (N.C.), Congaree National Park (S.C.).

2016	Florida (Daytona Beach, Pompano Beach, Fort Lauderdale, West Palm Beach, Palm Beach, Lake Worth, Washington Oaks Gardens, St. Augustine); Beaufort; Charlotte & the South Mountains; Caw Caw Plantation; Anderson & Greenville, S.C.; England (London, Plymouth, Falmouth, Penzance, St. Ives, Cornish Coast), Wales (Lamphey, Pembrokeshire Coastal Path, Tenby, Fishguard, Holyhead), Ireland (Dublin, Enniskerry, Wicklow Mountains), Scotland (Edinburgh).
2017	Jekyll Island, St. Simon's Island, Brunswick, Ga.; Walterboro, S.C.; Charlotte, Crowder's Mountain, N.C. and Camden, S.C.; Providence and Newport, R.I., Cape Cod, Provincetown and Boston (Mass.); Wilmington and Southport, N.C., Stafford and Arlington, Va., Washington, D.C.; Charlotte (again), Pisgah National Forest (Daniel Ridge Loop), Congaree National Park; Beaufort (twice).
2018	Charlotte; Asheville & Winston-Salem (NC); Beaufort; Utah: Salt Lake City, Bryce Canyon National Park, Capitol Reef Nat. Park, Arches Nat. Park, Canyonlands Nat. Park, Kodachrome State Park, Dead Horse Point State Park, and Monument Valley (Ariz.); Caw Caw Plantation.
2019	Hawaii (Kauai & Oahu: Honolulu, Lihue, Poipu, Waimea, Eleelee, Koloa) and Australia (Sydney, Melbourne, Cairns, Clifton Beach, Palm Cove, Kuranda, Port Douglas, Frankland Islands and the Great Barrier Reef, Phillip Island), Los Angeles; August Road Trip: Charlotte & Roan Mountain (N.C.) with Nunnenkamps), Knoxville (the Hortons), Mammoth Cave National Park (Ky.), Cumberland Gap & Cumberland Gap National Historical Park, Charlotte again (Harriett & Morgan), Easley (S.C., Dan & Janet Conover); and Beaufort.
2020	Savannah & Tybee Island. Then it became the Year of the Pandemic.
2021	Beaufort; N.C. Jaunt: Wilmington and Gloucester, Nags Head and Kitty Hawk (Craig Nuckles); Garden City Beach (S.C., Archie Biggs); House sitting at Folly Beach (June, Oct); Caw Caw Plantation; Waxhaw (Nunnenkamps) & N.C. Mts Jaunt 2: Burnsville (Crafts Fair), Mt. Mitchell, Asheville and Arboretum hike (Leslee), Croft State Park hike (S.C.); California: Morgan Brynnan (Sacramento, Chico, Redding) and the Jenner-Point Reyes-Big Sur run (San Rafael, Monterey, Pacific Grove, Carmel-by-the-Sea, etc.); Waxhaw (again).
2022	Le Roade Tripple III (Midwest Ramble): Milwaukee, Madison and Taliesin (Wis.), Dubuque (Iowa), Bloomington (Ill.), Indianapolis (Ind.), Knoxville (Tenn., and Hortons); Beaufort (S.C.), Brevard (N.C. and hiking) Fall getaway; Charleston Tea Garden.
2023	Greensboro, N.C. (small group High School Reunion)

Other Travels

1950-1965 – Travels with family (Chicago, St. Louis, New York World's Fair, etc.)

1966 – New York City, Washington, D.C., Ocean Drive Beach (S.C.)

1967-71 – Maxton, Wingate, Charlotte, Chapel Hill, Durham, Red Springs, Richmond

1972 – New York State, Montreal

Addendum C – Travel

1971-1979 – Washington, D.C., New York, Baltimore, Atlanta, Philadelphia, Pittsburgh, Houston, Tampa/St. Petersburg, Orlando, Tallahassee, Cincinnati, Cleveland, Columbus (O.), Jacksonville (Fla.), New Haven, Mobile, Baton Rouge, Richmond, Buffalo, Norfolk, Portsmouth, Chesapeake, Williamsburg, Virginia Beach, Roanoke, Newport News and Hampton (Va.), Athens (Ga.), Macon (Ga.), Birmingham (Ala.), Charleston (W.Va.), Lexington (Va.), Darlington (SC), Daytona Beach, St. Augustine, College Park (Md.), St. Bonaventure (NY), etc. – all as a sportswriter.

Natural Areas Visited (North America)

Great Smoky Mountains National Park	Shenandoah National Park
Rocky Mountain National Park	Grand Canyon National Park
Crater Lake National Park	Yosemite National Park
Glacier National Park	Yellowstone National Park
Congaree National Park	Grand Teton National Park
Olympic National Park	Redwoods National Park
Mt. Rainier National Park	Zion National Park
Everglades National Park	Acadia National Park
Mesa Verde National Park	Death Valley National Park
Sequoia National Park	King's Canyon National Park
Carlsbad Caverns National Park	Big Bend National Park
Guadalupe Mountains National Park	Theodore Roosevelt Nat. Park
Bryce Canyon National Park	Capitol Reef National Park
Arches National Park	Canyonlands National Park
Mammoth Cave National Park	Cumberland Gap Nat. Hist. Park
Timucuan Preserve National Park	Banff National Park (Canada)
Waterton National Park (Canada)	Yoho National Park (Canada)
Glacier National Park (Canada)	Adirondack Park
Mt. Revelstoke Nat. Park (Canada)	Cumberland Island Nat. Seashore
Mt. St. Helens National Monument	Giant Sequoia National Monument
Vermillion Cliffs Nat. Monument	Monument Valley (Ariz.)
Grand Staircase-Escalante Nat. Monument (Utah)	Point Reyes Nat. Seashore (Cal.)
Muir Woods National Monument (Cal.)	Sumter National Forest
Pisgah National Forest	

As Luck Would Have It

Nantahala National Forest	Oregon Dunes National Seashore
Sleeping Bear Dunes National Lakeshore	Pictured Rocks Nat. Lakeshore
Cape Cod National Seashore	Chattahoochee National Forest
Uwharrie National Forest	South Mountains (NC)
Francis Marion National Forest	San Juan National Forest
Olympic National Forest	Rio Grande National Forest
Lincoln National Forest	Bridger-Teton National Forest
Croatan National Forest	Sierra National Forest
Sequoia National Forest	Kaibab National Forest
Stanislaus National Forest	Inyo National Forest
Pike National Forest	San Isabel National Forest
Arapaho National Forest	Roosevelt National Forest
White River National Forest	Grand Mesa National Forest
Hiawatha National Forest	Geo. Washington Nat. Forest
Monongahela National Forest	Uncompahee National Forest
Jefferson National Forest	Franklin Mountains (Texas)
Cape Hatteras Nat. Seashore	Pea Island Nat. Wildlife Refuge
Weminuch Wilderness Area	Okeefenokee Swamp (Ga.)
Blue Ridge Mountains	Shenandoah Valley (Va.)
Providence Canyon (Ga.)	The Oregon Coast
Florida Keys	Sangre de Cristo Mountains
Snowmass Wilderness Area	Champlain Islands (NY/Vt)
Eagle's Rest Wilderness Area	The Coast Range (Cal.)
Antelope Canyon (Ariz.)	Marble Canyon (Ariz.)
Horseshoe Bend (Ariz.)	Amargosa Range (Cal.)
Hunter-Fryingpan Wilderness Area	Lake Huron (Mich.)
Lake Michigan	Lake Superior
Panamint Range (Cal.)	Lee Vining Canyon (Cal.)
Mono Lake (Cal.)	Santa Cruz Mountains (Cal.)

Addendum C - Travel

Merced River (Cal.)	Manatee Springs (Fla.)
The Appalachian Trail (NC, Va, Ga, Tenn, SC)	Luray Caverns (Va.)
Bahia Honda Beach (Fla.)	Mojave Desert (Cal.)
Old Santee Canal (SC)	Tuolumne River (Cal.)
Lake Kenyaha (Cal.)	Cranberry Wilderness (W.Va)
Mackinac Island (Mich.)	New River Gorge (W.Va.)
Biddle Knob (W.Va.)	Kure Beach (N.C.)
Lynches River (SC)	Falls of Hill's Creek (W.Va.)
Santee Coastal Reserve (SC)	Chattahoochee River (Ga.)
Grand Island (Mich.)	Colorado River (Colo., Ariz)
Rio Grande River (Ariz./Texas)	St. Lawrence River (Quebec)
King's River (Cal.)	Don Pedro Lake (Cal.)
Lake Powell (Ariz.)	Big Talbot Island (Fla.)
Continental Divide Trail (Colo.)	The Alleghenies
The Cascades (Wash.)	The Front Range (Colo.)
The Berkshires (Mass.)	Pike's Peak (Colo.)
The High Sierras/Sierra Nevada Range (Cal.)	San Juan Mountains (Colo.)
Squaw Valley & Lake Tahoe	The Ozarks (Ark.)
Great Falls & Mather Gorge (Va.)	Cloudland Canyon (Ga.)
Mount Desert Island (Me.)	Donner Pass (Cal.)
Columbia River Gorge (Ore./Wash.)	Multnomah Falls (Ore.)
Raven's Cliff Falls (SC)	Whitewater Falls (NC)
Quinault Rain Forest (Wash.)	Hoh Rain Forest (Wash.)
Plum Island (Mass.)	Flathead National Forest
Bridal Veil Falls (NC)	Linville Falls (NC)
Lake Quinnault (Wash.)	Lake Placid (NY)
Lake George (NY)	Lake Lure (NC)
Lake Jackson (Fla.)	Blue Mountain Lake (NY)
High Rock Lake (NC)	Bull Island (SC)
Guana Lake (Fla.)	Matanzas River (Fla.)

As Luck Would Have It

Governor's Creek (Fla.)	Ponte Vedra Beach dunes (Fla.)
Potomac River (Va.)	Waterrock Knob (NC)
Whiteside Mountain (NC)	Clingman's Dome (Tenn.)
Saranac Lake (NY)	Lake Marion (SC)
Lake Moultrie (SC)	Big Schloss (Va.)
Lake Chatuge (Ga.)	Lake Burton (Ga.)
Mount Jo (NY)	Baker Mountain (NY)
San Luis Valley (Colo.)	Mississippi River
York River (Va.)	James River (Va.)
St. John's River (Fla.)	Yadkin River (NC)
Ausable River (NY)	Ausable Chasm (NY)
Edisto River (SC)	Peedee River (NC/SC)
Grandfather Mountain (NC)	Black Mountain (NC)
Tallulah Gorge & Falls (Ga.)	Pee Dee River (SC/NC)
Lake Waccamaw (NC)	North Anna River (Va.)
Graveyard Fields (NC)	Gorges State Park (NC)
Caw Caw Plantation (SC)	Jones Gap State Park (SC)
Crowder's Mountain State Park (NC)	Big Bend Ranch State Park (Tex)
Rosillos Mountains (Texas)	Chisos Mountains (Texas)
Guadalupe Mountains (Texas)	Sierra Del Carmen Mts (Tex.)
Selkirk Mountains (Canada)	Coast Mountains (Canada)
Lake Moraine (Canada)	Lake Louise (Canada)
Columbia Mountains (Canada)	Little Missouri River (N.D.)
Tahkenitch Creek, near Oregon Dunes	Blowing Rock (NC)
Kodachrome Basin State Park (Utah)	Henry Mountains (Utah)
Dead Horse Point State Park (Utah)	Wasatch Mountains (Utah)
Manti-La Sal National Forest (Utah)	Dixie National Forest (Utah)
Fishlake National Forest (Utah)	La Sal Mountains (Utah)
Red Canyon (Utah)	Tropic Canyon (Utah)
Waimea Canyon (Kauai)	Na Pali Coast (Kauai)

Addendum C – Travel

Daniel Boone National Forest	Roan Mountain (NC/Tenn)
Croft State Park (S.C.)	Mt. Mitchell State Park (NC)
The Sutter Buttes (Cal.) **	Big Sur Coastline (Cal.)
Sutter Nat. Wildlife Refuge (Cal.)	Los Padres Nat. Forest (Cal.)
Santa Lucia Mountains (Cal.)	Ohio River (Ind., Ky.)
Milwaukee River (Wis.)	Lake Mendota (Wis.)
Wisconsin River	Lake Monona (Wis.)
DuPont State Forest (N.C.)	Wind River Range (Wyo.)
The Selkirk Mountains (Can.)	The Adamant Mountains (Can.)

** *The smallest mountain range in the world.*

Plus various state parks and state forests in NC, SC, NY, Fla., Va., Ga., Cal., Mass., Ariz., W.Va., Ore., Colo., Wash., Tenn., Ala., Utah, Wyo., Mich., Nev., Mont., Texas, Minn.,Wis., N.D., Hawaii.

NATURAL AREAS ABROAD

The Italian Alps	Canadian Rockies
Kruger National Park (South Africa)	Drakensberg Range (SA)
Blyde River Canyon NP (SA)	Cape Point NP (SA)
Table Mountain NP (SA)	Mathaga Game Ranch (SA)
Sea Point & Camp's Bay (SA)	Devil's Peak (SA)
Boulder Beach (SA)	Cape Peninsula NP (SA)
St. Lawrence River (Canada)	Charente River (France)
Isle Mujeres (Mexico)	The Yucatan (Mexico)
Blue Mountains (Jamaica)	Negril reefs (Jamaica)
Rose Island (Bahamas)	Chub Cay (Bahamas)
The Blue Grotto (Italy)	Lake Maggiore (Italy)
Isle of Capri (Italy)	Sierra Nevada range (Spain)
North Mountains (Japan)	Glacier Nat. Park (Argentina)
Thira caldera (Santorini, Greece)	Montmorency Falls (Quebec)
Laurentian Mountains (Quebec)	Wicklow Mountains, Ireland
Pembrokeshire Coastal Path, Wales	Cornwall Coastal Path, England

Glendalough Valley, Ireland	Snowdonia Nat. Park, Wales
Perito Moreno Glacier (Argentina)	Fitz Roy Range (Argentinian Andes)
Phillip Island (Australia)	Great Barrier Reef (Australia)
Normanby Island Nat. Park (Australia)	Frankland Islands (Australia)
Kuranda Tropical Forest (Australia)	Barron Gorge National Park (Australia)

GREAT DRIVES

Pacific Coast Highway, from Jenner to Point Reyes, Monterey to Big Sur (Cal.)	Blue Ridge Parkway (Va., N.C., Tenn.)
Hudson Highlands (N.Y.)	Adirondack Park Ramble (N.Y.)
Utah Ramble	The Florida Keys
Capetown to Cape Point (South Africa)	Guadalupe to Big Bend (Tex.)
Going to the Sun Road (Mont.)	Many Glacier to Aspen to Durango (Colo.)
Calgary to Vancouver (via Banff)	

CULTURAL TREASURES VISITED (through 2023)

Museums and Galleries

The Louvre, Paris	Centre Georges Pompidou, Paris
British Museum, London	The Tate Modern, London
Victoria & Albert Museum, London	Apsley House (Duke of Wellington's estate), London
Vatican Museum, Rome	Doges Palace Museum, Venice
Murano Glass Blowing (gallery), Venice	Effizi Palace, Florence
Galleria dell'Accademia, Florence	Columbus' birthplace, Genoa
Metropolitan Museum of Art, New York	Museum of Modern Art, New York
American Natural History Museum, New York	Art Institute of Chicago
Chicago History Museum	Museum of Fine Arts, Boston
Isabella Stewart Gardner Museum, Boston	The Guild of Boston Artists Gallery
The Getty Center Museum, Los Angeles	Los Angeles County Museum of Art, Los Angeles

Addendum C - Travel

The Smithsonian Institution, Washington, D.C.: National Air & Space Museum Museum of Natural History The Freer Gallery The National Portrait Gallery	The Smithsonian Institution, Washington, D.C. The Museum of American Art The National Art Gallery Washington, D.C. The Renwick Gallery
Corcoran Gallery, Washington, D.C.	The Phillips Collection, Washington, D.C.
The National Archive, Washington, D.C.	U.S. Marine Corps Museum, Washington, D.C.
National Archaeological Museum, Athens, Greece	Museum of Cycladic Art, Athens
Acropolis Museum, Athens	The Benaki Museum, Athens
Museum of Attica History and Civilization, Athens	Museum of Prehistoric Art, Fira (Santorini)
Kyoto National Museum, Kyoto (Japan)	The Prado, Madrid
Reina Sofia, Madrid	Thyssen-Bornemisza, Madrid
Museo Arqueologico, Seville	Royal Palace & Gardens, Seville
The Mezquita, Cordoba	The Alhambra, Granada
Museo de la Americas, Barcelona	Museo Picasso, Barcelona
Museu d'Art Contemporani, Barcelona	Museu d'Historia de la Ciutat, Barcelona
Fundacio Fran Daurel, Barcelona	La Pedrera, Barcelona
Poble Espanyol (historic village replica), Barcelona	Museo de Nacionale de Belle Artes, Buenos Aires
The Van Gogh Museum, Amsterdam	The Rijksmuseum, Amsterdam
The Anne Frank House, Amsterdam	Deutsches Museum, Munich
Pinakothek der Moderne, Munich	Alta Pinakothek, Munich
Neue Pinakothek, Munich	The Residenz (palace), Munich
National Gallery of Ireland, Dublin	National Museum of Scotland, Edinburgh
Scottish National Gallery, Edinburgh	Edinburgh Castle, Edinburgh
Holyrood House Palace, Edinburgh	Art Gallery of New South Wales (Sydney, Australia)
The Museum of Contemporary Art (Sydney, Australia)	The National Gallery of Victoria (Melbourne, Australia)
The Ian Potter Centre for Contemporary Art (Melbourne, Australia)	The Victorian Arts Centre (Melbourne, Australia)
Musee National des Beaux-Arts, Quebec City	Cuivres D'Art Albert Gilles, Sainte-Anne (Quebec)

As Luck Would Have It

The Vancouver Art Gallery (British Columbia)	Victoria Art Gallery, Bath (England)
Barbara Hepworth Gallery, St. Ives (England)	Denver Museum, Denver
The High Museum of Art, Atlanta	Bass Museum of Art, Miami Beach
Pacific Science Center, Seattle	New Orleans Museum of Art
Ogden Museum of Southern Art, New Orleans	Contemporary Arts Center, New Orleans
A Gallery for Fine Photography, New Orleans	Milwaukee Museum of Art, Milwaukee
Chazen Museum of Art, Madison (Wis.)	Taliesin East (Frank Lloyd Wright museum), Wisconsin
Dubuque Museum of Art, Dubuque (Iowa)	Museum of Science, Cambridge (Mass.)
Clark Art Institute, Williamstown (Mass.)	Williams College Museum of Art, Williamstown (Mass.)
Cape Cod Museum of Art, Dennis (Mass.)	RISD Museum of Art, Providence (R.I.)
Hunter Museum of American Art, Chattanooga	Peabody Place Museum, Memphis
The Parthenon (recreation), Nashville	Knoxville Museum of Art (Tenn.)
Will Rogers Museum, Claremore (Okla.)	El Paso Museum of Art (Tex.)
National Museum of Wildlife Art, Jackson (Wyo.)	North Carolina Museum of Art, Raleigh (N.C.)
North Carolina Museum of Natural Sciences, Raleigh (N.C.)	Museum for Contemporary Art and Design, Raleigh (N.C.)
Wright Brothers Nat. Memorial Museum, Kill Devil Hills (N.C.)	North Carolina Maritime Museum, Southport (N.C.)
New Mint Museum of Art, Charlotte (N.C.)	Mint Museum of Art, Charlotte (N.C.)
Mint Crafts Museum, Charlotte (N.C.)	Bechtler Museum of Modern Art, Charlotte (N.C.)
Cameron Museum of Art, Wilmington (N.C.)	Outer Banks Museum, Buxton (N.C.)
Ackland Art Museum, Chapel Hill (N.C.)	Reynolda House Museum, Winston-Salem (N.C.)
Southeastern Center for Contemporary Art, Winston-Salem (N.C.)	Museum of Early Southern Decorative Arts, Winston-Salem (N.C.)
Old Salem Village (N.C.)	Society for the Four Arts Gallery, Palm Beach (Fla.)
Cultural Council of Palm Beach County Art Museum (Fla.)	Armory Art Center, West Palm Beach (Fla.)
SCAD Museum of Art, Savannah (Ga.)	The Gutstein Gallery (SCAD), Savannah (Ga.)

Addendum C – Travel

Jepson Center for the Arts, Savannah (Ga.)	Ships of the Sea Maritime Museum, Savannah (Ga.)
Gibbes Museum of Art, Charleston (S.C.)	Charleston Museum, Charleston
International African-American Museum, Charleston	Mace Brown Museum of Natural History, Charleston
Halsey Institute of Contemporary Art, Charleston	The City Gallery, Charleston
Redux Contemporary Art Center, Charleston	Patriot's Point Naval & Maritime Museum, Mt. Pleasant (S.C.)
South Carolina State Museum, Columbia (S.C.)	Columbia Museum of Art, Columbia (S.C.)
Florence County Museum of Art, Florence (S.C.)	Greenville County Museum of Art, Greenville (S.C.)
Bob Jones University Museum & Gallery, Greenville (S.C.)	Morris Museum of Art, Augusta (Ga.)
Laurel and Hardy Museum, Harlem (Ga.)	Museum of Northern California Art (Chico, Cal.)
California State Railroad Museum (Sacramento, Cal.)	Great Lakes Shipwreck Museum, Whitefish Point (Mich.)
Demmos Art Museum, Traverse City (Mich.)	Jacksonville Museum (Fla.)
Mariner's Museum, Newport News (Va.)	The Torpedo Factory Art Center, Alexandria (Va.)
Anasazi State Park Museum & archaeological dig (Utah)	Moab Museum of Film & Western Heritage (Utah)
Colleton (County) Museum, Walterboro (S.C.)	South Carolina Artisans Center, Walterboro (S.C.)
Tamarack Craft Center, Beckley (W.Va.)	Kentucky Artisan Center, Berea (Ky.)
North Bennett Street School of Crafts, Boston	Biltmore Mansion, Asheville (N.C.)
Carl Sandburg House (N.C.)	Flannery O'Connor House, Savannah (Ga.)
Historic houses of Charleston & elsewhere	Monticello (Virginia)
Mount Vernon (Virginia)	Colonial Williamsburg (Virginia)
Powerscourt Estate, Enniskerry (Ireland)	Swan House/Atlanta History Center, Atlanta
Castillo de San Marcos National Monument, St. Augustine (Fla.)	Transylvania Heritage Museum, Brevard (N.C.)
Fort Fisher Historic Museum, Kure Beach (N.C.)	Drayton Hall, Charleston (S.C.)

As Luck Would Have It

Middleton Place, Charleston (S.C.)	Fort Sumter, Charleston (S.C.)
Fort Moultrie, Charleston (S.C.)	Boone Hall Plantation (S.C.)
Hampton Plantation (S.C.)	Old Santee Canal Museum, Moncks Corner (S.C.)
Charles Towne Landing museum, Charleston (S.C.)	... And scores of private (for profit) galleries in various cities of the world.

GARDENS

Bois de Boulogne, Paris	Keukenhoff Gardens, Lisse (Holland)
The English Garden, Munich	The Gardens of the Alhambra, Granada, Spain
Butchart Gardens (Vancouver Island)	National Arboretum, Washington, D.C.
Dumbarton Oaks, Washington. D.C.	Central Park, New York
Jardi D'Escultures (sculpture), Barcelona	National Garden, Athens
Jardín Botánico, Buenos Aires	Sydney & Walda Bestoff Sculpture Garden, New Orleans
Hyde Park, London	Gyllyngdune Gardens, Falmouth, England
Barbara Hepworth Sculpture Garden, St. Ives, England	Powerscourt Gardens, Enniskerry, Ireland
St. Stephen's Green, Dublin	Royal Botanic Garden, Edinburgh
Royal Palace & Gardens, Seville	Royal Botanic Gardens, Melbourne
Royal Botanic Garden, Sydney	Hyde Park, Sydney
Boston Public Gardens	Boston Common
Olbrich Gardens, Madison (Wis.)	Hirshhorn Sculpture Garden, Washington, D.C.
Philip Hulitar Sculpture Garden, Palm Beach (Fla.)	Society of the Four Arts Botanical Garden, Palm Beach (Fla.)
Grandview Gardens, West Palm Beach (Fla.)	Dr. Sun Yat-Sen Classical Chinese Garden, Vancouver (B.C.)
Stanley Park Rose Garden, Vancouver (B.C.)	The Shakespeare Garden, Vancouver (B.C.)
Botanical Gardens at Roger Williams Park, Providence (R.I.)	Cape Cod Museum (sculpture garden, Dennis (Mass.)
River Gallery Sculpture Gardens, Chattanooga (Tenn.)	Magnolia Gardens, Charleston (S.C.)
Middleton Place Gardens, Charleston (S.C.)	Audubon Swamp Garden, Charleston (S.C.)
Hampton Park, Charleston (S.C.)	White Point Gardens, Charleston (S.C.)

Addendum C – Travel

Brookgreen Gardens (sculpture) (S.C.)	Edisto Gardens (S.C.)
North Carolina Arboretum, Asheville (N.C.)	Elizabethan Gardens, Manteo (N.C.)
Washington Oaks Gardens (Fla.)	Charleston (Oregon) Gardens
Mepkin Abbey Gardens (S.C.)	Cypress Gardens (S.C.)
Charles Towne Landing (S.C.)	Swan House Japanese Garden, Atlanta
Meadows in the Sky, Mount Revelstoke, British Columbia (Canada)	Riverbanks Gardens (at the Zoo, Columbia S.C.)
Falls Park on the Reedy, Greenville (S.C.)	Gardens at the Knoxville Museum of Art
Various gardens in Japan (...and numerous private gardens, such as the Tom and Lib Nunnenkamp's world-class Japanese Gardens, The Maple Walk in Charlotte N.C. and Pearl Fryar's topiary garden in S.C.)	

FAMOUS RUINS

The Colisseum, Rome
Roman Forum, Rome
Palatine Hill, Rome
The Acropolis, Athens
Hadrian's Arch, Athens
Temple of Hephaestus, Athens
Temple of the Olympian Zeus, Athens

Temple of Poseidon, Cape Sounion (Greece)
Pompeii (Italy)
Chichen Itza (Mexico)
Tulum (Mexico)
Mesa Verde cliff dwellings, Colorado
Wicklow Graveyard (Ireland)
The Bishop's Palace, Lamphey (Wales)

GREAT CHURCHES, CATHEDRALS, TEMPLES & SHRINES

The Vatican, Rome
St. Peter's Cathedral, Rome
Notre Dame, Paris
St. Patrick's Cathedral, New York
Cathedral of St. John the Divine, New York
Basilica di Santa Maria del Santo Spirito The Duomo), Florence
The Mezquita, Cordoba
Sagrada Familia, Barcelona
Cathedral S. Maria Nascente Duomo, Milan
Cattedrale di San Rufino, Assisi
Tōdai-ji (Eastern Great Temple), Nara, Japan
Kiyomizu Temple, Kyoto
Kinkaku-ji (The Golden Temple or pavillion), Kyoto
Kiyomizudera Temple, Kyoto

Chion-in temple, Kyoto
Notre Dame Cathedral, Quebec City
Notre Dame des Victoires, Quebec City
Basilica Sainte-Anne-de-Beaupre, Sainte-Anne (Quebec)
Frauenkirche - Cathedral Church of Our Lady, Munich
Theatinerkirche St. Kajetan, Munich
The Old – New Synagogue, Prague
The Basilica of St. Peter and St. Paul & Vysehrad Cemetery, Prague
The Saint Louis Cathedral, New Orleans
Kapnikarea, Athens
The Church of the Holy Apostles, Athens
Cathedral Basilica of St. Augustine (Fla.)
St. Paul's Cathedral, Melbourne

As Luck Would Have It

FAMOUS BUILDINGS, TOWERS & BRIDGES

The Parthenon, Athens
The Colisseum, Rome
The Pantheon, Rome
Eiffel Tower, Paris
Empire State Building, New York
Statue of Liberty, New York
Leaning Tower of Pisa (Italy)
The Capitol, Washington, D.C.
Space Needle, Seattle
John Hancock Building, Chicago
Library of Congress, Washington, D.C.
Big Ben, London
Parliament, London
Buckingham Palace, London
Chrysler Building, New York
La Scala Opera House, Milan
Boston Public Library, Boston
The Residenz, Munich
Sydney Opera House, Sydney
The Harbor Bridge, Sydney
The Golden Gate Bridge, San Francisco
Chesapeake Bay Bridge-Tunnel
Mackinac Bridge, Michigan
Charles Bridge, Prague
Ravenel Bridge, Charleston (S.C.)
Shijo Bridge, Kyoto
Wisconsin State Capitol, Madison
Sundial Bridge at Turtle Bay, Redding (Calif.),

GREAT ZOOS & AQUARIUMS

London Zoo, England
Lincoln Park Zoo, Chicago
Montreal Zoo, Canada
Buenos Aires Zoo, Argentina
Jacksonville Zoo, Florida
North Carolina Zoological Park, Asheboro (NC)
Riverbanks Zoo, Columbia (SC)
Greenville Zoo, S.C.
Charles Towne Landing Animal Forest
Monterey Bay Aquarium
Seattle Aquarium
Montreal Aquarium
Audubon Aquarium of the Americas, New Orleans
North Carolina Aquarium, Kure Beach
Charleston Aquarium (SC)

MEMORIALS

Mayflower Arch, Plymouth (England)
Wright Brothers Memorial, Kitty Hawk (N.C.)
Lincoln Memorial, Washington, D.C.
Jefferson Memorial, Washington, D.C.
Arlington Cemetery (Va.)
Rhodes Memorial, Capetown (South Africa)
Sir Walter Scott Memorial, Edinburgh
Washington Monument, Washington, D.C.
Korean War Memorial, Washington, D.C.
Vietnam Memorial, Washington, D.C.
U.S. Air Force Memorial, Washington, D.C.
Chickamauga and Chattanooga National Military Park (Tenn./Ga.)
U.S.S. Yorktown, Mt. Pleasant (SC)
U.S.S. North Carolina, Wilmington (N.C.)
Fort Dorchester State Historic Site (S.C.)
Charlestown Landing State Historical Site (S.C.)
The Pilgrim Monument, Provincetown (Mass.)

Addendum C - Travel

GREAT HOTELS

The Ritz, Paris
The Drake, Chicago
Adams Mark, New York
Alvear Palace Hotel, Buenos Aires
The Roosevelt, New Orleans
Chateau Frontenac, Quebec City
Grove Park Inn, Asheville (N.C.)
The Greenbrier, White Sulphur Springs (W.Va.)
The Cloister, Sea Island (Ga.)
The Mark, San Francisco
Hotel Triton, San Francisco

The Bellagio, Las Vegas
Regina Palace, Lake Maggiore, Stressa (Italy)
The Sagamore, Lake George (N.Y.)
Fairmont Chateau Lake Louise, Banff, Alberta (Canada)
Prince of Wales, Waterton National Park, Alberta (Canada)
The Queen Elizabeth, Montreal (Canada)
The Mills House, Charleston (S.C.)
The Francis Marion Hotel, Charleston (S.C.)
Charleston Place Hotel, Charleston (S.C.)
The Peabody, Memphis (Tenn.)

STADIUMS and ARENAS (*covered team as beat sportswriter)

I covered games as a sportswriter in almost all of the listed stadia & arenas, including for four years as beat writer on the Washington Redskins and the (then) Baltimore Colts; three years as football beat writer on the University of Georgia Bulldogs; three years on the Jacksonville University Dolphins beat; three years on the ODU Monarchs; a year on the Hampton Institute Pirates beat; and a year on the Christopher Newport College Mariners beat.

The Coliseum, Rome (no lions at the time)	The Original Yankee Stadium, New York (Yankees)
Shea Stadium, New York (Jets, Mets)	Madison Square Garden, New York (Knicks)
Fenway Park, Boston (Red Sox)	Wrigley Field, Chicago (Cubs)
Comisky Park (new), Chicago (White Sox)	The Astrodome, Houston (Oilers, then)
Memorial Stadium, Baltimore (Colts*)	Veterans Stadium, Philadelphia (Eagles)
RFK Stadium, Washington D.C. (Redskins*)	Three Rivers Stadium, Pittsburgh (Pirates, Steelers)
Riverfront Stadium, Cincinnati (Bengals, Reds)	Tampa Stadium (old, Buccaneers)
The Omni Coliseum, Atlanta (Hawks)	Tiger Stadium, Baton Rouge (La.) (LSU)
Neyland Stadium, Knoxville (U. of Tennessee)	Ohio Stadium, Columbus (Ohio State U.)
The Yale Bowl, New Haven (Conn.)	The Gator Bowl, Jacksonville (Fla.)
Reynolds Coliseum, Raleigh (N.C. State)	Carter-Finley Stadium, Raleigh (N.C.) (N.C. State)

Carmichael Auditorium, Chapel Hill (N.C.) (UNC)	Kenan Stadium, Chapel Hill (N.C.) UNC
Cameron Indoor Stadium, Durham (N.C.) (Duke)	Greensboro Coliseum, Greensboro (N.C.)
Sanford Stadium, Athens, Ga. (Univ. of Georgia*)	Richmond Coliseum, Richmond (Va.)
Charlotte Coliseum, Charlotte (new)	Charlotte Coliseum, (old)
Jacksonville Coliseum, Jacksonville, Fla. (Jacksonville Univ.*)	Dudley Field, Nashville (Tenn.) (Vanderbilt)
Cole Field House, College Park (Md.) (Univ. of Maryland)	Hampton Roads Coliseum, Hampton (Va.) (Virginia Squires)
Scope, Norfolk (Va.)	Roanoke Coliseum (Va.)
Harbor Park, Norfolk (Va.)	Metro Stadium, Norfolk (Va.)
Memorial Stadium, Clemson (S.C.) (Clemson)	Williams-Brice Stadium, Columbia (S.C.) (USC Gamecocks)
Roberts Municipal Stadium, Evansville (Ind.)	Commonwealth Stadium (Univ. of Kentucky)
Peninsula Memorial Park, Newport News (Va.)	Old Dominion University Fieldhouse Norfolk (Va.) (ODU*)
Zable Stadium, Williamsburg (Va.) (William and Mary)	Johnson-Hagood Stadium (The Citadel)
McAlister Fieldhouse (The Citadel)	Sam Wolfson Baseball Park (Jacksonville Suns)
The Baseball Grounds of Jacksonville, Jacksonville (Fla.)(Suns)	North Charleston Coliseum, North Charleston (S.C.)
Joe Riley Park, Charleston (S.C.)	College Park, Charleston
Also: *Norfolk State, Randolph-Macon, Hampden-Sydney, VMI, Marshall, St. Bonaventure, George Mason, Hampton Institute, Christopher Newport, etc. (basketball arenas), Washington & Lee (football)*	

Acknowledgments

Apart from the many people I've already mentioned as being keys to whatever success I've had in work and life, there are others I wish to thank for their roles in bringing this book to fruition.

First my parents. Without them, no life. No book.

Second, Mary B. Johnston, memoir coach, writer and friend, not only for her savvy evaluation of and suggestions for the manuscript, but for convincing me this enterprise wasn't a dumb, ego-driven idea and that it could have value.

Third, my great compadre Wesley Moore (a.k.a., the Bard of the Beach), for being the first "beta" reader of the book, for his clear-eyed suggestions, and for counseling me to approach any and all revisions with more engagement (I was ambivalent in the beginning, and it showed, especially in the first chapters).

Fourth, Vally M. Sharpe, editor and creative director of United Writers Press, for her admirable book design and guidance on printing.

Last, Rosemary Michaud, and all my other friends who encouraged me to chronicle my life so far. They were right. It's been a lot more fun than I anticipated. And I'm grateful.

Sine qua non, as always.

About the Author

BILL THOMPSON was for 42 years a reporter and editor with *Newport News (Va.) Daily Press*, the *Jacksonville (Fla.) Times-Union* and the *Charleston (S.C.) Post and Courier*. Since his semi-retirement in 2012, he has worked part-time as a freelance writer and editor.

Over the course of 53 years, he has been a sportswriter, music columnist, features writer, book review editor, business and consumer writer, film critic and columnist, travel writer-editor and arts writer. Currently, Thompson contributes articles on the arts to a variety of print and online publications. His book reviews appear regularly in *Kirkus Reviews*, the *Los Angeles Review of Books*, and *The Post and Courier*, with whom he also continues to publish travel pieces. Born in Asheboro, N.C., he has resided in Charleston since 1980.

Thompson's previous books include *Art and Craft: 30 Years on the Literary Beat* (University of South Carolina Press), *Why Travel: A Way of Being, A Way of Seeing* (Sojourner Books), and *Lightwaves: A Film Critic's Odyssey* (Sojourner Books). He is a member of the National Book Critics Circle.

As Luck Would Have It is his (mostly) earnest memoir of a life and a career in journalism.